Acknowledgments

We are, as a planetary body, experiencing a time of profound unprecedented change. The making of *Family of Light* changed my life—sometimes with shocking suddenness, although for the most part, change crept in slowly, undetected initially, yet gradually unfolding and shifting my awareness and perceptions of myself and the world around me. The creators of *Family of Light* are the Pleiadians—my wise, witty, and wondrous friends who began working with me over ten years ago. It is they who are to be acknowledged first and foremost for the energy and insight they share in this book. And just who are the Pleiadians? Truthfully, I don't really know, although whoever they are, they have taught me the value of living. For their love, guidance, and inspiration, I am eternally grateful.

Many people are to be acknowledged for their hard work, love, and support in bringing this book to fruition. I especially thank my sister Karen for her outstanding contributions to my lessons in living; for her dedication to both myself and the Pleiadians over the years, and most of all for transforming her own life. For choosing to be alive and well, and available to complete this book, Karen, you have my utmost thanks, respect, and love.

To Susan Draughon and Rose Bissonnette, I extend my heartfelt thanks for your participation in receiving the tales, for holding the energy, and living the book.

My editor at Bear & Company, John Nelson, deserves a very special accolade. His editorial finesse, patience, determination, and endless hours of hard work were a major contribution in the production of *Family of Light*. My deepest appreciation, John, for your abilities, as well as my admiration for your personal dedication to holding the energy and transforming your life.

My gratitude and thanks to Barbara and Gerry Clow for their inspiration, faith, and patience with this project. My thanks as well to the staff at Bear & Company—Jody Winters in publicity, Diane Winters in foreign rights; to Pooter, Amy, Chris, Karen, Rob, and Bob. To everyone at Bear, I truly appreciate the spirit of your support.

In addition, I thank Laurel and Marty Carlson for their essential computer assistance, Wendy Warner and Erin MacMichael for tape transcription, Sonya Moore for proofing, Melinda Belter for interior design, and Sarah Honeycutt for interior art. The captivating cover art is once again by artist Peter Everly, whose work graces my previous books. Thank you, Peter, for the many makeovers! And my thanks for the splendid cover design by Gaelyn Larrick and her staff at Lightbourne.

Lastly and most importantly, I offer a tribute of thanks to all of the people who assisted me over the years, to my readers and tapelanders, and especially my home group who have continued with playful dedication to rethink reality.

On behalf of myself and the Pleiadians—those enigmatic, elusive energy beings I call my friends—I offer our love and appreciation for the opportunity to serve our unique buffet of knowledge. Perhaps you too shall be changed by reading, then living, *Family of Light*.

Foreword

For over ten years a group of multidimensional beings—who call themselves the Pleiadians—have blended and merged their energies with my sister Barbara, creating a unique and engaging relationship. The infusion of the Pleiadian energy into Barbara's life, my life, and the lives of countless others has been marked by change. In addition, with the success of the Pleiadians' first two books, *Bringers of the Dawn: Teachings from the Pleiadians* and *Earth: Pleiadian Keys to the Living Library*, Barbara and I found ourselves overwhelmed at times by the abundance of mail we received. Over the years thousands of letters have arrived from people all over the world, and I have truly been astounded by the heartfelt response to the Pleiadian teachings. People write expressing their gratitude: to the Pleiadians of course, for the teachings brought forth, and to Barbara for receiving, distributing, and *living* these teachings. These letters depict a multitude of individuals, many seeking to make sense of a world seemingly on the brink of madness. So many of their messages expressed their deep-seated feelings as they shared with us their visions and dreams, triumphs and victories, anguishes and fears. They told us that they felt more galactic than human, and many of them spoke of feeling connected to the star system called the Pleiades, and to our amazement over and over again so many of them said, "I know I am a member of Family of Light." The Pleiadians say Family of Light are systems busters who travel through time to systems in need of change, helping to facilitate the collapse of these systems. It became so routine for a letter writer to proclaim Family of Light status that Barbara and I kidded about someday titling a book, *Family of Light.*

Everything comes around in its own time, and a few years back, as people began clamoring for another "P" book, we began discussing ideas for one. At one point we were sure that by the end of 1996 a new book would be ready for publication. It wasn't. However, Halloween of 1996 arrived, and with the moon in Cancer, Barbara and I set out to energize the inception of this book. In the evening darkness with candles, crystals, and clear intentions, we conducted a ceremony in my circle garden, with the object of calling in the energies that would be assisting us in the process of creating this work.

This latest Pleiadian book would be different than the first two in that the Pleiadians would channel each specific chapter. Barbara's intention was to conduct book channelings on auspicious dates, such as new and full moons, and to receive all the necessary book material from the P's by spring equinox 1997. Our first session took place on a winter evening in mid-January at Barbara's home. Our friends Susan and Rose along with myself would be the holders or keepers of frequency as Barbara channeled the Pleiadians. As the P's entered our reality for the initial book session, they were immensely pleased that the process was at last underway. Their first deed was to ask each of us women to reach to comet Hale-Bopp, which at that time was in the sign of Capricorn and not yet visible in our night sky. They said, "Visualize a huge dome or bubble—a cascading fountain of moisture—that is like a liquid essence of healing. You are bathed in sunshine, and at the same time, you have this spray or fountain of energy that is around you. Picture yourself lying in the sun, completely relaxed, with this huge bubble—an orb of moving liquid light—surrounding you. Keep this image going, and at the same time contact Hale-Bopp." They asked us to hold these images, and in that way we would be beaming something of who we were to the comet, while at the same time holding open the frequency. Our initial book sessions were peppered throughout the winter season, and each time we converged we discussed the previous session's information, along with Barbara conducting ceremony and playing her gong. After the energies were invoked, invariably Susan, Rose, and myself would snuggle up on the sofas as the Pleiadians wove their tales into another chapter of the story.

If you have per chance interacted with the Pleiadian energy, then you know it is synonymous with change. This change is an adjustment on a frequency level and requires the shift to come from within. Change is oftentimes unpredictable, and the P's have said, "How you handle chaos is a test of your ability to evolve and change—change creates new experiences and this is how you learn." Each one of us involved in the initial phase of creating this book manifested a challenge for ourselves, our own personal dance with chaos and change. My own winds of change blew at me full-force about a month into the book channelings. I awoke one morning and couldn't get out of bed. We had scheduled a book session for noon of that day, and I called my sister to tell her I wasn't feeling well. That was an understatement; I was so weak, I literally couldn't move. Later that day, Barbara, Susan, and Rose came by my house to check on me, and it's a good thing they did because I spent the next three days in bed, oblivious to what was happening around me. My friends and family helped nurse me back to health, and before long I was feeling healthy and strong again. I was aware though that this crash was a big warning signal, as the right side of my body had ever-so-slowly started deteriorating a few years back. I was extremely stubborn though and had been shrugging this off; I believed that whatever it was, I could fix it myself. Hey, I was a spiritual being who believed she created her own reality; I wouldn't manifest a major malfunction in my body.

I do believe that my higher self guides me, and soon after I experienced my "crash," a series of synchronistic events unfolded in my life. As a result, around the time of the spring equinox, I found myself scheduled for a CAT scan. The results? A brain tumor. Shock, disbelief, and denial followed. "This is happening to me? Out of all probabilities and choices, I manifest this?" That evening, as I searched the heavens for a glimpse of comet Hale-Bopp, a feeling of acceptance started nudging at me, and I proclaimed to myself, "I will heal this." Invariably, that is what I set out to do. With a holistic healer, a bevy of herbal remedies, and a piece of equipment called a Photon Sound Beam, I made the intention to shrink my tumor within three months, by the summer solstice. In addition, I intended to work with the emotional body as well, searching deep within for clues as to why I would create a brain tumor.

The final chapter of the main body of this work, chapter twelve, was completed on April 22, 1997: Earth Day and a full moon. We were in fine spirits, and as the P's once again entered our reality, they said to us, "Chapter thirteen will come at a later time, you will know when the time is right, you will all agree upon it. You will cleverly wink at one another, with those witty winks, as the wild winds of change move around you. The appropriate time will manifest; there will be some conclusions, some bizarre, unique, unfathomable events to experience. Victories. For now though, we will continue in the modality of the story. Relax."

As our lessons in living unfold in these times of extraordinary acceleration and change, the Pleiadians have taught me that oftentimes the most difficult of challenges offer the most opportunity, and what we don't want to experience holds the biggest victory. At the end of June I scheduled another CAT scan and MRI. The results showed my tumor to be as large then as it was in March—the size of a baseball. "Wow, I didn't shrink my tumor, after all that energy I expended!" was my first thought when I was told the tests' results. For a few minutes I considered myself a failure. Rather quickly it became clear to me that a miraculous healing was not in the cards! Spirit had lessons for me to experience, that given a choice of a thousand probabilities, I would never have chosen. "OK," I said to my doctor, "if you would connect me with the brain surgeon you told me about, I would really appreciate it." Before the day was over, I was scheduled to have my tumor removed.

I was faced, no doubt, with the biggest fear and challenge of my life. Within a few days all my beautiful long hair would be shorn off and the top of my skull cut open. What a test! I remember the P's saying, "A crisis is an opportunity designed to shatter the patterns of rigid behavior trapped within." I surrendered and made the intention to face my ordeal with as much grace and ease as I could possibly manifest. Along the way I was able to set my fears aside and love became my biggest ally. I contacted everyone I felt connected to, asking them to send me their love and blessings. There were people I was terrified to call; however, I did and felt wonderful afterward. I opened to the love frequency and in return received an amazing outpouring of love from my family, friends, old acquaintances, doctors, nurses, and neighbors—everyone. I faced my challenge fortified with love and emerged from a five-hour operation with flying colors.

My post-operative healing process offered me the opportunity to uncover, comprehend, and transmute some of the behavioral patterns that imprisoned me. Now, fourteen months after my "cranial lift," as the P's call it, I look and feel like a new person. Yes indeed, sometimes we need to be shaken to the core of our being to change.

I trust in sharing my story with you—my lessons in living

—that as the winds of change intensify in your life, you will pause to remind yourself that everything life has to offer is a lesson. Play the game of life with gusto, and please remember to choose love and turn all of your encounters into lessons of loving opportunity.

A special thanks to my sister Barbara and the Pleiadians for their love, support, and friendship.

Karen Marciniak
September 1998

Introduction by the Pleiadians

Greetings, dear friends. It is our distinct pleasure to partake of your reality once again, and to journey with you for a while on the road to adventure and self-discovery. "What journey?" you may rightly ask, for it may seem that you are traveling in circles, and the idea of a great adventure in your life is a far cry and distant dream from the daily dogma and relentless burdens of living you face. Nonetheless, allow us to accompany you for a while, as companions offering to entertain you and enliven your step as we point out the sites and symbols along the way.

We are storytellers extraordinaire, or so we've been told, and we too have traveled in seemingly endless circles, so we have much in common. Our destination is the same as yours, for we are you in another version and form of reality, as deeply entrenched and entrapped as you believe yourselves to be. What sort of paradox is this? And who indeed are we, claiming kin to you and yours? And why do we desire to journey with you? Well, these things you must decide for yourselves.

We relate great tales and relish a resplendently irreverent good humor, all intended to figure things out, in all due respect, as best we can. We strive to make sense of existence, gathering multidimensional pieces of a puzzle into a form and shape that encompass untold and unrecognized societies. "How can pieces of a puzzle be multidimensional and what is multidimensional anyway?" We can hear your questions now, and we guarantee that you will have many more before the journey is complete.

So we ask, may we join you and enter your reality by invitation? For it is through your beckoning and with your permission that we spring forth as a part of your life. Feel into the depths of your being before you respond. Seek inside for an answer, for to invite us into your reality as friends and companions will with certainty confound and change your lives, and perhaps some of you are quite content with where you are. Perhaps you are not really interested in multi-dimensional realities and perceive these ideas as vague notions and tidbits of unfounded fiction, fracturing and fragmenting a logic you paid so dearly to achieve. If that is the case, then you may do well to stop short now, and put our tale aside. Perhaps in another time and place, we will meet again. If, however, we have piqued your curiosity and you feel compelled to continue, so be it.

It is best to start with the truth. As a matter of fact—if there is such a thing—it is best to end with the truth as well. "And how about the middle and all along the way?" you may ask. Well, the truth is essential throughout the journey; however, the ongoing paradox invariably involves your point of view. Remember that. Now we are travelers through time, which is the best way to describe us. We call ourselves Pleiadians, though we answer to many names and characters. We are as real as you believe yourselves to be. When we encounter you, we meet ourselves located on a slice of time, poised, as you believe, in a solid physical 3-D world. You fascinate us, and perhaps by the end of our travels and tales, you will be fascinated with yourselves as well. For now the task of telling is at hand, and so the tale begins.

FAMILY OF LIGHT

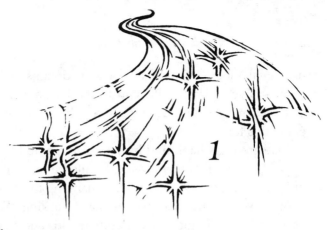

Reality Exists
as a Mirror

From our point of view, we are storytellers and are very pleased to have the opportunity to enter your reality, whether you are hearing our voices, reading our words, or are so finely tuned that you can listen to the silence of a summer's afternoon and hear our whisperings, echoes, our voices on the breeze. So, however you encounter us, it is our great pleasure to have your attention for a while.

We are Pleiadians, or this is how we address ourselves; however, from your point of view, we are as difficult to name as you are from our point of view. You may appear to know yourselves; you have names, addresses, and certainly numbers that identify you. Perhaps shortly you will be chipped and programmed: hologrammed, automated, and turned into robotized beings. You are headed in this direction. Do you know who you are?

We are a collective of energies, conscious and alive. We call home a small cluster of stars in the heavens known to you as the Pleiades. This cluster of stars has held a dear and important place in many cultures all over the globe, and some of you have traveled there or have wished to travel there or have remembered these stars in your dreams. Many native people have claimed a kinship to the Pleiades and to other star systems as well, since we are certainly not the only players in this tale.

We are Pleiadians, and by some are reputed to be similar to you in form. By others we are reputed to be kin to reptiles, or blue in color, or shape-shifters, changing from one form to another. What is the answer? you may be asking. Well, we certainly find our home outside your world, and yet we are a part of your world. You are kin to us, and as kin we would like to share our perspective with you. As we view your world, we have the ability to look at time as if it is an ongoing diary and to pick any point in time and pursue it. This is not such an easy task, you know. There are those who hunt points in time, whose sole ambition is to locate places in time and enter into them. They are, by profession or aspiration, time-jumpers, which is a concept that your world, late-twentieth- and early-twenty-first-century Earth, is learning to grasp.

There is an energy that is coming to your world now in massive waves, and in forms that are completely unrecognizable at this time, according to how your visual acuity is tuned. However your other senses relay that you are living in the most absurd of times. Everything is topsy-turvy! You are in the collapse of your civilization, and this is why, as relatives—multidimensional beings related to you—we are here. Specifically, we want to share with you our perspective of what is occurring on your world. We think of ourselves as teachers and students, comrades and friends, and certainly as renegades. We like to define ourselves as systems busters and to seek out those in the Family of Light who are systems busters as well. We are all Family of Light, and all of you drawn to our words and energy know about Family of Light. You are one of us, and perhaps have heard our tales and wonder about their origin. We will tell you now about these tales, about what is happening to you.

As you live from day to day you wonder what is happening. Why is everything changing? Why is everybody going berserk? What does this mean? Why are deceit and lies the name of the game? Where is moral integrity? Where is responsibility? Where is reliability? Where is compassion? Where is friendship? Where is love? Where is marriage, partnership? Well, where are they? In a culture that is collapsing, in a culture that is turning itself upside down, these qualities are not there. You live in a time when you are pioneering a new territory, when a massive shift in perception will occur, and when the wealth of an age is upon you. When you gather that wealth, you will discover that what you gather will be your ability to shift your perceptions. This is why we are here at this time.

In our aspiration to explore and wonder who we are and why our world is the way it is, we have discovered a way to reach into your world, the world that you call Earth. The world you live in is where a version of your attention is focused; however there is so much more of you that you have not as yet met and explored. Our intention, in these most absurd of times, is to point out to you that these absurdities have a reason: You are about to shift from a very rigid, linear, restricted, and controlled way of living and expressing yourselves into an opening of perception, like a fan spreading open, to greater expression and function.

Our intention is to jiggle your consciousness. You are much more than you have ever been told. Even to those of you who have studied widely, considering yourselves adepts in the areas of mysticism, spirituality, shamanism, and the occult, we still say to keep your innocence, your humility, your respect, your reverence, and your purpose for living always available to expand. Without those attributes and with all you must now know, you will be blinded by your own light and closed off. This is, of course, the test that the absurdity of the times creates for all of humanity. Will you be able to shift your perceptions?

Look at the various areas of life where it appears that your freedoms are becoming very restricted. You cannot freely express yourself or voice your opinion, and you must follow like sheep, doing what you are told. Money means nothing any more: Automobiles are thousands and thousands and thousands of dollars; everything is priced outrageously high, from education to communication. Your homes are threatened. Can you afford your homes? Where will you get your food? It costs so much money to have fun these days. Children no longer play with sticks and stones or mud because they are afraid of the earth.

You are told there are diseases everywhere, and so you have become terrified of your body, which has become rigid and closed down. Your relationships with friends, family, and loved ones are falling apart. The understanding of sexuality is at its darkest hour. The misuse of sexual energy, by way of perversion and occult power through sexual abuse, has become rampantly open now and is understood as a tool of the ruling classes whether they are popes, priests, or presidents. Perhaps pharaohs and patriarchs and a number of other "p's" can be included in that category as well. Your religions, educational systems, and leaders no longer make sense, and they are devoid of compassion. Their vision of humanity is cold; it is not a warm vision. The New World Order is certainly not a warm fuzzy.

The great waves of energy that move through your systems are changing each of you on a physiological level. You are being changed as a planet. This is why we, as Pleiadian kin, come to you now. As we sought to know more about ourselves, we found avenues to meet you. We began to understand that by meeting and working with you and placing a wedge of energy and attention into your world, we could understand ourselves. If there is anything we have learned in our journey through existence, it is the certainty that *reality exists as a mirror*. Some of you will say, "Ah, yes, we know that, we have heard it before in many many terms: What you put out is what you get back. Thought creates. You create your own reality." At this point this is a very deep and important concept to grasp, for it is truly one of the greatest continuing laws of existence.

We knew that if reality always mirrored itself and if your portal of Earth drew us, there must be something here. Over the last ten years, in your time, we have been learning about you, teaching you, coming into your world and disseminating information that would assist you at a very crucial point in your development: *where your civilization collapses.* You may ask yourself, "Why, pray tell, is this happening?" And some of you may deny this and say, "Civilization is not collapsing. Look, I have a bigger car, more money, perfumes and leather shoes, cashmere sweaters, trips all over the world—more than ever before." Oh, that is true. Some people are sitting in the lap of luxury at this time. However, if you were to open your eyes and take a look around, you would see very few who live this way. The vast majority of people in your world have signed up for a struggle. By this we mean that they believe what they are told. They attend school, listen to their parents, or to whatever authority is extending its truth and saying, "This is how it is." Although there are many reasons for such compliance, this is a characteristic of humanity, or at least one that has occurred for a long period of time.

And yet, if no one has told you, dear humans, you are some of the most powerful forces tucked away in the universe's secret caches. We do not say this to get you all stirred up and certainly not to expand your egos; when you are powerful, you can destroy yourselves as easily as you can create universes. The reason we are here addressing the subject of the absurdity of your times and the fall of your civilization is because you are taking power and destroying yourselves, rather than creating universes. Many forms of life know about this power because the universe is vast, and the galaxy is abuzz with consciousness. Many of you know that you are connected to star systems that hold intelligent life, and that on all the planets of your solar system intelligent life exists in some form or another. Your solar system is not what it appears to be. The planets, as orbs of energy, exist within a particular relationship to one another, and they are planned in the same way you plan your automobiles. You do not randomly throw things together and then expect them to take you from one place to another. You have developed an understanding of certain principles and built an expanded science around the process—a science that appears to work because you believe in it. You have designed it because you are powerful creators; however, if you stick to that one science, you may miss another science and then another and another and another, for there is certainly more than one science. Reality is a mirror, and anything you decide to create can work if you believe in your power and have a few tricks up your sleeve! Our intention is to offer you a few tricks of the trade, a few lessons in living so that you can move through these most tumultuous times.

As Family of Light, you are systems busters who travel through time entering systems in need of change. You go in and facilitate the collapse of systems because you carry light. Now we ask you to question light, to ask where it comes from. How many shapes does it have? What does it do besides light your homes and streets? When light changes shape or color, when it flashes across the sky, does it shift your consciousness? When the eclipses of the sun or the moon in the afternoon or night sky hold you captive, what really happens in your being when light is altered from its normal patterns? Light, from one point of view, is information.

As we share our light with you, we will engage in a mind-to-mind exchange to extend your field of perception, to explore the corridors of time through your DNA in order for you to remember the real history of your planet and yourselves. You have been taught that early humans crawled out of caves or were expelled from the garden, and they slowly evolved over a few thousand years, struggling with ice ages and discovering the wheel. This is certainly not the case. You spring from an ancestral heritage that comes from the stars. You are stellar stock, and you and your planet are not here as the result of a "big bang" accident. Everything is planned, and the universe runs because it is planned. Perhaps you cannot conceive of the engineer, the designer, or the production staff; however that does not mean they do not exist. When you were children, there were many things you could not imagine. Even now as you fledgling adults are reaching for more, there are all kinds of stellar punctuation marks occurring in the heavens, which you cannot imagine, altering your consciousness month by month as you move into the twenty-first century. Actually we are making an energetic opening for you to reach into the twenty-first century by assisting you to become beings of value, purpose, and complete responsibility.

Your challenge at this time is to gain your freedom, and this does not mean fighting the government, the military, their mind control, or any of the other forces that appear to trap you in 3-D. Although it may appear as if you are being squeezed and your individuality annihilated, there is always a bigger picture. In dealing with day-to-day living, you may find yourself questioning your sanity, your purpose, and what to do from moment to moment, overwhelmed by the whole spectrum of life. We will say to you that the picture is bigger than you can imagine, so buckle up and relax. Life on Earth includes much more than you thought, so do not get stressed out now, for there is much more to come. Our intention is to help you get through these times; ideally we will create openings of energy through you, so you can relax and understand who you are in this immense process of change.

You may be asking yourselves, "Why are we Pleiadians

here, why do we do this?" Well, we can tell you this: We learn
from you, then learn about ourselves because reality is a mirror. You are not easily looked up on the map of existence. Can
you imagine all of existence and time being simultaneous?
How then do you imagine one finds you, a quarter of a mil-
limeter of a needle in a cosmic haystack? Well we have found
you in the search to know ourselves, and we experiment with
you because we understand that you and all of existence are
an experiment. Everything you do is a reflection of what you
believe, so it is our intention to disseminate energy as ideas
that you, as humankind, can perhaps use as tools for survival.
It is a handy term, "tools for survival." And this is what you
must survive: the shift from linear living into a multidimensional expression, where the fan goes from closed to open—
like the ones that geisha girls and Southern ladies carry.

This is not an easy process to undergo; therefore we will
address some of the most difficult areas. You must keep your
physical, emotional, mental, and spiritual bodies tuned up,
and there are many ways to do this. Now here is something of
importance for us to convey to you: Whenever you are fin-
ished living on the Earth, you have a chance to review your
life, to look back and say, "Hmmm, look what I did on Earth."
We would be most pleased to hear you say that you had gathered many golden nuggets of lessons in living, and in that
regard, we would like to contribute a form of gold to you.
However this gold is more than a valuable mineral to exchange at the bank for material riches. It would be too easy for
you if we were able to arrive with a truckload of gold and
dump it in your backyard, saying, "Here, dear humans, is
your golden light. Go cash this in." Many of you would like to
just be given your truths, as you sit on your thrones and say,
"Look here, I deserve it."

Remember, as Family of Light, you go into systems to create change. You are wayshowers, and oftentimes you must
learn the most difficult aspects of the system before you can

change it. You enter a system to experience its depths in excruciating detail so that you can relate to others—your family and friends. Although the rest of the world may not think they are Family of Light, they all are. Everything is part of one and the same. The story we tell is the story of humankind, a story of living in the cosmos as a huge family, a family that has had its problems as all families do. This family has a branch, which we will call Family of Dark. As Family of Light, one of our intentions is to explore Family of Dark with you, the branch that hides out in the closet, the branch that everyone is ashamed of, humiliated over, and embarrassed by. To add to the confusing mix of names, labelings, and misunderstandings, your branch of Family of Light, the systems busters, is often considered to be the black sheep by both sides of the family!

As you experience the massive opening of energy, which is indeed an infusion of light, an equal experience of looking at the dark cannot be avoided. In the world of duality where you dwell, shadow defines light, just as it does in photography. It may be that the more light you create the more you will see the shadow that defines it. Perhaps some of you have been a bit naive, too willing to play the game, listening to those in authority and doing what you are told rather than thinking for yourselves. People are not encouraged to think. Mass programming is in effect all over the world. You are taught what to think, and you pay a good amount of money for this experience. This type of misuse of energy can only go so far before people become disconnected little boxes, compartmentalized fragments without a connection to the whole. When anything becomes fragmented in this way, it eventually collapses on itself. The part cannot stay separate from the whole for very long; only for a little while can a small part remain isolated. Do you understand? When you look at Nature, plants, animals, or yourselves, you see that you cannot reproduce if you remain isolated. Because you have been fed a series of falsehoods for thousands and thousands of years, each person on Earth has become compartmentalized in what he or she believes, disconnected from real thinking and from the self and other people. At the foundation of your worldview is the idea of separation, which is not necessarily the wisest of founding principles.

As light and cosmic energy arrive to affect your planet, this founding principle will begin to collapse like an ancient infrastructure built in an improper place. Structures can be viewed from the future, you know, so as to consider the generations to come. Your ancients built structures on the planet in this way that have lasted far longer than your modern buildings will, because they had a broader understanding of the cosmos. They were in contact with the heavens as well as with the Earth, and they were motivated by the idea that everything is alive. They considered ether, representing spirit and the invisible realms, as a fifth element in addition to earth, air, fire, and water.

We use this invisible realm to come from the Pleiades to speak to you, to electrify you, to have fun with you, to learn from you, and to transmit an energy that is yours back to you. When we look at your world from our point of view, you exist as if on a page in a book. In many ways we look you up, knowing what comes before and what goes after you. Living on the page, you have no idea, in most cases, of this broader perspective. You believe you know what happened before your time; however you do not have the full, juicy version. When we first located you, we felt that we could assist you to perhaps enhance the pages of your book.

Now, there are beings who exist within a very limited mode of thought, who feel that, when they write a book on existence, the book must stay fixed forever. From your point of view these beings may be called Gods. They exist in an abode of the Deity where they have a home of their own. Within their abode they have laws and regulations, which are far more expansive than yours but also of limited thought. This is how you became confused and surrendered your thinking in the first place. Beings that you adored, emulated, and did not question, have issued you laws that no longer further your well-being. The laws have never really worked; however, now with the mass compartmentalization of people, the gears of old Earth laws are grinding your civilization to a screeching halt. This may be seen in part as people lose jobs and have greater credit card debt than they ever had. In the process of moving faster and faster to expand yourselves and accommodate this shift in energy, you are losing touch with practical living and common sense. We said earlier that your freedom is at stake. Your freedom is based upon your response-ability—two words—your ability to respond to what is happening in your world. If you cannot manage 3-D, you will never make it in Multi-D.

Many of you think managing 3-D requires going faster, having more technology, knowing more people, and rushing here and there. As things go faster, slow down and put yourself at ease. Take time to listen to the birds, the sounds of Nature, the crackling of a fire—the natural sounds. Get outdoors. Be by yourself. Take time for yourself and learn to expand your awareness and to hear a voice inside. Then be certain to question that voice and all that the voice brings. When you begin to open the fan of yourself, with respect to these voices in your head, an opening to the abstract occurs. Humankind has long been deflected from thinking in abstract, nonlinear terms. Living nowadays is quite solidified and linear. Yet you rob yourself of a great venue of experience, a necessary frontier for masses of you to become artists within. Many many people must create a new high art of thinking in order to translate the changes that are coming. The ancient Egyptians called the voice in the head the *Ka*. It was considered to be a double, or another version of the self used for guidance and inspiration. This concept is very different from the idea of possession.

For now we want to set a tone of inspiration and inform you that on this journey with us you are to activate this mysterious concept called the Ka. Because you no longer experience or seek out the abstract, this little-known aspect of human development has been forgotten. Yet the abstract knocks on your door today, asking you to reach beyond yourself. In many ways the Internet mirrors the linkup of your inner psychic highways and byways. Reach for guidance. Reach for your inheritance because this voice, the Ka, this inspiration is yours. You must learn to claim your inheritance in this most absurd of times. The Ka will help you to shift between linear and multidimensional living. It is an important key to knowing yourself, an essential tool for survival. Do not forget it.

As your system collapses and familiar comforts disappear very rapidly in the next few years, there will be an equal amount of opportunities and reappearances. A force of psychic spiritual energy will explode, creating many rapid changes on a planetary scale. These changes will herald a new way of thinking and perceiving, where you will link up as one humanity. For a while it will look like the linkups are happening on the Internet, where up to a certain point in time it will appear that you are more and more electronically linked. Many of you holdbacks and electronic teetotalers will slowly creep forward and decide to get an Internet connection. However, because of unknown plans, great energy surges and geophysical Earth changes are occurring at a rapid rate, and your electronic grids will break down. Many of you will find yourselves in the situation of here today, gone tomorrow. Will there be electricity? Will there even be food and water? As this decade closes some of you will have one- or two-week bouts without a ready supply of food, electricity, and water. Changes may then begin to accelerate. Everything you do now, every day in every moment, counts.

You have been told that life is an accident and holds no meaning. We are telling you the exact opposite: The Big Engineer in the sky makes everything work, otherwise life comes to a screeching halt, and if and when that happens, it just means an overhaul is taking place. This is what is happening in your world: You are getting an overhaul, which does not imply that everyone's life will come to a halt. It means that whomever or whatever you have placed in positions of authority—be they governments, religious leaders, educational systems, kings, priests, popes, or presidents—their power will now be questioned. This is a time when power will return to the people.

You will have to claim for yourself attributes that few know about. Remember, in the cosmic annals you are seen as extraordinarily powerful beings, as creations of the Gods. You are the ace up their sleeve, created genetically eons ago and stored away, tucked away for that just-in-case time, and in many ways you have been secreted in the corridors of time. In the Big Book of Existence, it is hard to find you; however you have been found. Your time coordinates are known, and now many are coming to your world because they all know there is a vein of gold here, and some will trick and entice you with their distractions.

Be very selective of what you choose to think, and believe in yourself as you unfold your fan of consciousness. Perhaps you will then understand that the great infusion of energy from the heavens is going to shine on a pot of gold inside of you. As Family of Light, you are quite simply decoding and unfolding to what is already inside you, and as your family and kin, we will keep you company for a while and remind you of this process. We will support and encourage you, be good friends, and perhaps occasionally offer a shoulder to cry on, for the tears you will shed unveil mysteries and deeper feelings—no tears of pity or blame though, for they are foolish tears. The unveiling tears are healing, and you may experience them again and again as you read our words and experience life. Hold no shame over these tears because they help melt away the rigid control that has kept you from thinking and understanding who you are.

The power you have within you was given to you by the Gods when they wove your DNA together eons ago. You will now have to figure out why the heavens are full of visitors. Who are they? Are they the creator Gods? Extraterrestrials, aliens, and other forms of intelligence are coming forth through every version of reality. You are going to live with this experience, although the idea that other forms of intelligence can readily appear anywhere at any time will totally shatter your linear worldview. Remember, your linear world is based on a calendar, one that is not very old; and even an ancient calendar like the Maya's is still a time construct. Time is actually organized and constructed around a theme, which is set into motion and then remains consistent enough to create a thoughtform that maps it and makes a virtual reality. Time is elastic, and your experience of time is certainly not the same as the time we Pleiadians experience. We can scan the Book of Time and travel through time by picking coordinates. Time-jumping. You must understand this concept, then learn to become a time-jumper, first in your mind, then literally. The corridor is open, and it is important to understand that every lesson and experience in day-to-day living is to help the decoding of yourself as a galactic resident, and, most important, as a human being. At this time your most important task is to live. Do you understand? To want to live and to create a continuity in living will be in itself a challenge, for the more you live and are open to knowing many things, the more you are going to find out.

This wave of energy is waking you up psychically, triggering a perceptual shift, which makes you aware of so much more on many different levels. One of the greatest challenges you face is to understand how the mind works. We said that we will convey thought to you, mind to mind. You are, of course, telepathically expanding. Many people are very good at it while some people cannot imagine it ever working, yet you are born with this ability. If you cultivated it, you would be far more astute than you believe yourselves to be. Then again, if you were far more astute, you would not be as manageable. Much is kept from you and held in secret as higher knowledge: your ability to heal, to use your mind to create what you want, to send and receive messages, to see pictures or read energy fields—these are your innate abilities. If you claim these powers, then the few who live in wealth and are in charge will have a very difficult time managing you. How could they if you were free, unencumbered by shoulds, sins, and limitations?

As we have said, the abode of the Deity is the home of limited thinking. The Deity, or that which you worship, always gives you limited thinking so you can be managed. The Gods cavorted in the heavens, gallivanted around the universe, came to Earth to mate with the daughters and sons of humans, and then they left. Your literature is full of these stories. They left their kin, their progeny, and their bloodline behind to rule. Their children did not necessarily relate to you humans, so they set up priesthoods and militaries to control you and make you obey. During the feudal times of the Dark Ages, humans were locked in many limiting forms, and you are still today, although the forms that lock you in are invisible. You are not tried by inquisitions, nor are you pilloried or burned at the stake. A very subversive way exists in which you are controlled, very covert—so covert that it is unrecognizable by a large majority of those who are quite happy to be told what to think. Now this is going to be very disturbing and hard for some people to integrate, yet it is one of your greatest opportunities. Sometimes the darkest challenges, the most difficult lessons, hold the greatest gems of light.

Mind control will first be understood on your planet from

the negative side, from a very very dark avenue. And from that understanding you will spring into a very great light, a new dawning in the art of thinking, birthing a renaissance of being. Many people will come forward and speak the truth about how the human mind is being manipulated. You may then begin to understand how the Gods have played the same game. And perhaps it is the Gods themselves who manipulate certain humans, who then manipulate the rest of you, who are in turn the sheep who obey, who are always on time, and who die according to the official rules. This is going to stop!

As you learn about how you have been controlled and influenced, you will see how easy it is to feed you data. Whether it is through electronic repetition or dark, black-occult misuse of power through sexuality, cannibalism, and murders, all kinds of ways exist to fragment and compart-mentalize humans. You must use your mind as a tool because it is a field where you create. As we have said, everything is a mirror, and that is one truth that we bring to you as we tell you tales of existence. Our ancestors learned that reality mir-rors to you what you are, so remember. Remember!

You are taught that you are alone in existence so that you will be more manageable. Isolated, you cannot compare your world to another. If you were to visit another world and dis-cover they had the same God, you might check to see how God treated that world compared to how you are being treat-ed. Perhaps you would find a different God there and decide you like that God better. Or perhaps you would find there was no God at all, that the people were Gods themselves. In isola-tion you are deprived of expanding your experiences. Focused in linear time, with very third-dimensional, tactile experiences, you have shut yourself off from your psychic connection. As children, if you had psychic and out-of-the-body experiences and were able to time-travel and see other vistas and other worlds, you were terrified that people would think you were crazy. You were afraid of being locked up or punished. Oftentimes you were told to hush up, not to say a word, because such things were not accepted. Why were they not accepted? Perhaps because that kind of power sets people free. For those of you who have had these experiences, it is time for you to value them, to realize that as Family of Light you are already rich. No one needs to grant you anything. You are already wealthy, and you can share that wealth with your fellow humans, your family.

You may feel you are Family of Light, a certain kind of renegade, part of a different group of people all wondering, "How did I come to Earth? I feel galactic, stellar. I feel universal. I have never felt at home here; my family was odd; I couldn't get into the regular practices of living. I always looked to the heavens, always saw creatures—they came to my room at night to visit me." Well, Family of Light has many strange tales to tell. Because many of the visitors are shape-shifters, you have not been able to categorize and name them, which is, of course, your 3-D linear approach. Your science says name it, label it, give it a genus and species, then dissect it to know it. With the collapse of civilization and the expansion of consciousness into multidimensional living, your perceptions are the tools you will use to dissect, know, label, explore, and list your reality. Your perceptions are derived from your feelings and your ability to be yourself, to own and trust yourself, and to say what you feel, even when it may be diametrically opposed to everyone else's opinion. You may be called the Devil Incarnate. You may feel like cow pies are being thrown at you. Sometimes that is part of being true to yourself, but as humans you have given this up.

As we see it, if Family of Light is now here on Earth claiming a home, then you are certainly going to electrify the whole planet with new energy. One day everyone will be thinking, in one way or another, that they are all Family of Light. Even your scientists will agree that matter is simply trapped light, which suggests that you are all Family of Light and are all related to Family of Dark. We will make certain, as we explore our stories, that we tell the reason why Dark does what it does, and why Family of Light may disguise itself as Dark or Dark may disguise itself as Light. Perhaps, as we speak of mind control, you may say, "Oh, it must be Family of Dark that is doing mind control to humans. Who else would do this? It could not be Family of Light, could it?" Now remember, we are asking you to question light. Who owns light? Where does it come from? How was it generated? What kind is it? What color? What flavor? What does it do? What temperature is it? How does it make you feel?

Our stories are really about healing because this is what you are here to do as Family of Light. Some of you think that you are stellar visitors here to educate others, to raise their vibration, and to say, "Hey, here's your system, it's collapsing. Here are some new ideas, and then we are out of here." For a while Family of Light has done this disappearing act, its members jumping from one place to another, often so involved in their assignments that they forget to live. Well, Family of Light, because you have been so involved in your assignments, we are here to remind you at this time to live like you have never lived before! In living you truly fulfill your assignment because in living there is doing, creating, and then experiencing what you create, receiving the richness. Unlike the farmer in the garden who grows fine produce, then picks, prepares, and cooks the crop, and then sits down at a magnificent feast to enjoy the fruits of that labor; you, as Family of Light, have forgotten to sit down often enough and feast. You are so busy doing and creating that you are forgetting the wealth of living, of being in the Now, the ultimate richness of being alive.

It is this richness we want to remind you that you are missing. Many of the lessons, the tasks and challenges you are now experiencing in day-to-day life, in your body, in your relationships, in dealing with the world, are about finding the value in living. What do you value? What is important? What is character? What do morals mean to you? What is integrity? Much of what we explore will be about your integrity, your responsibility, and how they are tied into your freedom as your world goes belly-up in these most absurd of times.

Doorways of Time

We share our point of view with you for many reasons. From Earth our home in the Pleiades looks as if it is far away, a mere speck and cluster of twinkling light. We are seven, though it has been said we are eight and that Earth is part of our sisterhood, part of our fold of knowledge. As our records and our ancestors have shown us, this appears to be true. You are connected to us from an ancient ancient lineage.

As Family of Light, you have many opportunities: You can link up through time as multidimensional beings; you can learn how to move the dial of your consciousness. Although a hand has many fingers, it is connected to something larger, a body, and that body is connected to something even larger. As Family of Light, you are challenged to make visible the invisible body to which you are connected. All of humankind is thus connected, but you do not realize it. Many people think they are only a solid, physical form and therefore only seek out what supports their physical form. You believe your ancestors struggled in this manner. Perhaps the stories that you have been told about the past are not exactly correct. Perhaps your ancestors, your bloodline, operated at a much higher level than you can even imagine. They certainly lived in a time that was less technologically oriented in your terms, although the tyrannies on the other hand were just as pervasive.

There has always been a battle for the human mind, but that battle merely reflects a more expansive struggle happening on a multidimensional level, where a battle for your soul is being waged. Your Christian stories speak of the Devil and Christ, the Son of God who came to save you, and unless you are quick-witted enough to question these stories, you will believe that you must be "saved." As we have pointed out, you are in this dilemma, the collapse of your civilization, because you have given up your freedom to think, to discern, and to decide what you want. This collapse is also occurring because you are afraid to feel. Your feelings are vast and all-powerful, yet for many of you they are crosses of shame. However, it is through your feelings that you can ascertain what you value.

To know what you want in your lives, what you as humans value, you will have to question "the System." The System rewards you when you follow its messages and its rules: You jump when its bells are rung, mindlessly agreeing to play its game for a paycheck, a vacation, prestige, and status. By going along, you abdicate your ability to think for yourselves. The test you face is one of power, so we will explore some of the positive—and not so positive—aspects of power, because there is no escaping power. Your value and your power have been undermined. Perhaps you have been taught that you are flawed, or that the Gods must intercede on your behalf. Well the Gods, those whose dance through the heavens has become the cosmic quickstep, are going to appear everywhere in the next fifteen years, and these Gods may offer to "save" you with their technology.

So as you seek to understand the absurdity of these times, look at what is important by applying your values to yourself. This is one of the most important messages we have for you:

Your bloodline is rich. Ponder our words for a moment, then contemplate this: "What could be in my genes?" Imagine a computer with data banks of stored information. If you push the proper button, a tremendous amount of data is available; however a computer only holds the information put into it. In many ways you are far more advanced than any computer you will ever create in third-dimensional reality. You are living biological constructs with a magnificent lineage, capable of an impeccable existence. There are, however, a few adjustments needed to get you up and running, insights that are rarely understood by humans.

Instead of applying tools for living, you have been enticed to back away from the most valuable aspects of yourselves. You have been baited and set up. In your history it looks as if you have had to struggle for many freedoms and to fight for the right to think. Actually much of the tyranny that has existed in your Western world was designed to control the dissemination of knowledge. And some of the greatest suppressors of knowledge have been the religious organizations of your world. In order to stay in power, they approved the seizure of lands, monies, lives, and literature. Thousands of people were burned at the stake, and many great libraries of knowledge were also burned in order to wipe out the mysteries. What were the mysteries that religious organizations, seeking to maintain their power, were so eager to wipe out? Why is your history so full of crusaders and missionaries traveling all over the world? Were they sent to save the heathen as you have been told? Perhaps there are more interesting stories hidden behind those campaigns. The energy we bring allows us to pass through the pages of time that transpire before and after your Now. These are not the same pages found in the, as yet unburned, libraries of your world; the literature still available there holds hardly a thread of the truth. It holds what the victors want you to know, what those in power want you to believe. Manipulation and deceit, murder, treachery, and heresy have been whitewashed and painted over, or made so boring with dates and facts that your history reads like a dull conglomeration of meaninglessness.

In order to truly know yourself, begin by taking a deep breath and acknowledging your body: Be who you are and you will discover that you are very much alive and are here to live. Now stretch your imagination to see your ancestors: your parents, grandparents, great-grandparents, and on back through time; we dare you to find an end to your bloodline. If you found an end to your line, you could not be, could you? And as you consider your lineage, imagine your ancestral blood and the genetic codes stored in your body at this very moment, the genes that we maintain are so valuable. Over time what has been passed through your genes? How far back through time can you reach in your mind?

As we convey our energy to you and your world, can you imagine that we have a Book and that you can access that Book? Use your imagination and allow yourself to experience the true multidimensionalness of your being as you read our words and simultaneously watch realities unfold from the core of your being. Our voice comes from many directions and places and speaks to your multidimensional selves. We offer you tidbits of knowledge, truths to entice you along, so you can begin to weave your memories together and know what has transpired on Earth because you remember being here. All of your training during the last few thousand years does not exactly assist you in that endeavor. Over two thousand years ago, another time of opportunity prevailed on Earth, a time where a change in season meant moving from one age to another. It was the Age of Pisces, and as always Family of Light was there to usher in this Age. Ages mark the beginnings of seasons, each with their own flavor; in actuality, the Ages define where the action is going to be.

During the Dark Ages and early centuries of the Piscean Age, particularly the first five hundred years, considerable ignorance and confusion prevailed. Many important books, such as the Christian Bible, were not formulated until a few centuries into this era. Different factions formed back then and argued over whose God was God and which book held the truth. If you explore the cells of your being and drift into another avenue of perception, perhaps you can remember what it was like. The clothes were different, the colors of the vegetation were brighter, and the sky hung overhead as if one could reach up and touch it. It was a different era with a stillness in the land that today, in late-twentieth-century Earth, you do not have. Your world is abuzz, humming with electronic energy even when you are in the midst of the bush. You have switched your world on and no longer know what silence is. But your other selves do, and it is to all of your selves which we speak, as your eyes read the words and your minds grasp the ideas we are conveying.

As the Piscean Age actually began to blossom, many souls were purposely sent to incarnate. Family of Light came, of course, to electrify that age, to imprint it, set it into motion, and lay a foundation. The Piscean Age is characterized by some as one of great enlightenment and passion, one of forgiveness and deep cosmic connection. We ask you to look back and see: Is that what has happened over the last two thousand years? In the progression of any age, you can get caught up with the hoopla of what is coming, and you can in any age, in any incarnation and in any place in existence, forget yourselves.

Whenever an age is opening or closing, a great shift of energy occurs. It could be considered like a change of political administrations, and as with a change of administration, there is always a shift of power. Now, one of the most vital forces you must understand is power. When you reflect on values and what you want to have, some of you think that power is money or money is power. *Knowledge is power.* And then consider that just because you have knowledge does not mean you are wise. How you use knowledge will determine what will happen with power. As reality continues to maintain the ongoing law of mirroring itself, how you use your power will determine what happens to you. This is very important for you to grasp. You cannot escape power and its lessons. As a matter of fact, everything being directed at you today is meant to make you feel powerless, to have you believe you have not one iota of power. And this belief, stored in the cells of your being, was imprinted thousands of years ago.

When the Piscean Age was beginning, many beings incarnated who had a quickening of abilities, and the rest of humankind seemed to marvel over them. These beings, both men and women, could heal people instantaneously because they understood cosmic laws. In those days the telegraph, telephone, television, or telecomputer did not exist; there was no device to quickly tell others what was happening. The "tele" system was word of mouth from one person to another. People did not travel far in those days, and few could read or write. Those with quickened abilities sprang up everywhere; they were healers and could perform miraculous feats, and so the land was abuzz for a few hundred years with this opening of energy. These beings spread out over the land that today you call the Middle East, an area that is very important in your planetary history. They were there to raise the frequency of the Piscean Age by inspiring people to step through this doorway of change into a new era. The heavens were full of "punctuation marks," just as the heavens today will be full of signs as you enter the twenty-first century. Beings and energies of light will be contrived and holographically projected onto the heavens, and some people will believe that it is the Second Coming of Christ, here to save you.

You are easily duped and tricked; however do not berate yourselves for what we share with you. It is our intent to read the Book to you as we see it in order for you to wake up. It is essential that you take charge of your lives and learn that life is significant, and that there are lessons to be learned in living. One of the most important lessons is for you to develop a sense of humor. So as we share the stories of your world with you, maintain a sense of humor and keep a perspective on the development of human consciousness. You are a consciousness that incarnates again and again, yet you now live as if your lives were meaningless struggles with disease, sickness, starvation, and war. And what about love?

You have all been touched by love at least once in your lives, and many of you come here over and over again just to experience love. When you find what is important to you, what is worth accruing, and list your values, we ask you to reflect for a moment: How important is love? Love comes in many many flavors and experiences. Love is the heart opening through an energetic connection between electrical fields that unites people, touching you in a way that never leaves you. As we look at the Book of Earth, we see over and over again that what moves you forward is this invisible force, this frequency that is called love. However some of you believe you are here to experience, to learn, to gather data, and to have a good time, and the importance of love is news to you. There is nothing wrong with these assumptions. Yet understanding the frequency of love is your ultimate lesson in living. To manifest it, all you have to do is feel it; however you know it is the hardest thing for you to do. Yet each of you comes here for love because nowhere else in existence is love as varied and rich, as unbounded, untethered, and unique as here on the fringes of the Milky Way Galaxy on what we call the Library of Earth.

So we ask you once again to consider what is in your genes. We refer to your world as the Library of Earth because libraries store data. If you are the most magnificent creatures here, far more advanced than all of your gadgetry and technology, then what is in those genes? Could it be the richness of the love frequency that is so vast, multifaceted, and priceless that no God wants it out there because it is "catchy?" Reflect on this for a moment. You know when you feel love it is quite contagious, is it not? Love spreads quite easily and is the opposite of fear. If you reflect upon fear and are truly honest with yourselves, you will see that many of the ideas instilled in you through your ancestral lineage, books, and history, are about fear. You are encouraged to be afraid of God and your bodies. You are convinced you must have an authority outside yourselves because you are not capable of managing your own biological beings. And now you are being convinced that even your local governments cannot manage you, that you need a larger global government to manage your world.

You must begin to manage yourselves as biological spiritual beings. Love is one of your major tools to living. How free you are with it, how self-generating and responsible, is the lesson that you have come into life to learn. Just as we ask you to question where light comes from, and what you do with it, we ask you to do the same for love. Where does love come from? Do you seek it outside yourselves? To whom or to what do you offer it? Do you ever think to give it to your Mother Earth or to the heavens? Do you think to give love to the molecules around you that constantly move in and out of your bodies? Your bodies are not solid; nothing here is. Everything is a dance of energy, an energy that is free and simply locks itself into shape and form because your perceptions are trained to see reality in a certain way and to continue a linear approach to existence. For example, every day each of you wakes up in the morning and faithfully reproduces yourself. You usually meet "you" in the bathroom mirror. You expect to see yourself because so much of reality is built on old expectations, conditioning, and training of the mind. Mind control takes many many avenues.

Limited thinking, encouraged and taught to your ancestors, is imprinted in the cells of your body. Your ancestors' responses to these teachings over thousands of years, and to the times in which they lived—their reactions to violence, laws, and authority—were imprinted in their bodies in the course of daily living. Everything you deal with in daily living is recorded and stored in your physical body, and just because you do not consciously remember your experiences does not mean the cells of your body forget. Memories and responses to living are passed through your genes from one generation to another.

Throughout the annals of Western history, you have passed down an imprint of fear. When Family of Light incarnated over two thousand years ago, they were adepts of Light and Love, capable of many miraculous feats, and those in authority felt threatened. They did not want these teachings brought to the masses, and so there were many opposing factions from the beginning. Some people attribute this awakening of consciousness to the birth of Christianity because of the stories about the character you now know as Jesus the Christ. He is, indeed, a composite character, compiled and designed over many many years. In actuality these are stories about Family of Light who came to the planet to bring truth, to challenge the system, and to disrupt a tyranny at that time when there was a potential for great change.

The character of Jesus was created to attribute these spectacular powers to one supernatural being. Imagine what could have happened with the knowledge of self-healing and with the idea that as you think, so shall it be. If people had started implementing these practices very quickly, what would have happened? Certainly the Roman Empire did not want subjects more powerful than their rulers. The Roman Empire was the Piscean version of the New World Order— a karmic parallel of the Aquarian Age. Both orders, old and new, offer the possibility for a domineering, world-conquering force. When you manage people, you must first convince them they need managing. So you create the problems and then let the people cry for solutions. Fear is distributed throughout the land—not love, which was the message of Family of Light. Fear has a very powerful vibration, and when one holds fear in the body it transmits everywhere rather quickly with the same "catchiness" as love.

There was a battle over love and fear. If love had prevailed, then the people would have understood their higher powers: the ability of the human mind to transcend the body, to astral travel, and to feel connected to All That Is. If that had occurred, then humans would have ended their separation. Well it was not to be. In the last two thousand years, you have moved deeper into separation rather than deeper into unity and love. Fear won. If you question this conclusion, we ask you to open the fan of history and see how many people have died in the name of a higher power. How many books have been burned and how many people have been raped and tortured? How many indigenous lands have been wiped out and ancient manuscripts destroyed?

An out-of-control energy, seeking power over others, came over the land. The books and works of the Great Ones who walked the planet were hidden. However Family of Light did not simply walk the area of the Middle East; they traveled widely. The world was not as confined as you have been told; even North America had been known for a long time as a very sacred land. Atlanteans brought much of their knowledge to this continent, and ancient artifacts from prehistory will be discovered in your modern era. Actually they have already been discovered but have been hidden away. Egyptians and many travelers from the Middle East and the Far East, including the Chinese, came here. The world in ancient times was navigated quite well. Family of Light was well-traveled and carried messages far and wide. This is why to this day many native cultures have stories of peacemakers from across the seas, who offered knowledge of higher vibrations and showed what was needed to live in harmony.

You may be thinking about this prospect: What do I need to have in order to live in harmony? It seems you require money in the bank, an automobile, clothes, and a roof over your head. It is true. Your world is designed in this way at this time. However, many of the things you count on today will be gone tomorrow, especially if you are not living in sync with cosmic law. If you already know that your thoughts affect everything and that you create your own reality, then rest assured that your version of reality will not simply disappear. However, those who refuse to acknowledge this law will have a sudden awakening. To seek an authority outside yourself is to dance in the abode of the Deity where limited thinking is the name of the game. As you experience everything being turned upside down, an opportunity is at hand to reprioritize your life. There is a strength inside you derived from your awakening to your own value, to what you are worth.

We can see the great waves of energy coming to your world, affecting you from many different points of view. There are stories written about the various choices you make, so do not think there is only one line of existence from which to choose. Each of you, in every moment, creates a probable world based on what you want and what is important to you. From our point of view, we see that the web-of-life will help you assign great meaning to your life so that you can get the best mileage, so to speak, out of this existence. If you wish to take the high road, the scenic route, then we suggest that you travel with love, a love that can only arise from inside you. And as you love and value yourself, it will become easier for you to love your lineage. Extending love to your ancestors will assist you in understanding their fears, as well as the immensity of the project you have undertaken. This project is so vast and spans such eons of time that the ages of which we speak, a few thousand years in each season, are mere pinpricks in time and existence. At these doorways of time, energy is always accelerated in order to build a new foundation.

In the coming era of the Aquarian Age, the energy coming through will seek to enlighten all humankind. In order for this to occur, you must understand the depth of your past, your karma, and the lessons in living of the Piscean Age that you are about to conclude. You must make sense of the last two thousand years and spread the awareness to humanity.

A veil has been laid like a thick and heavy fog over your consciousness for many reasons. When you were born most of you immediately felt the struggle of living. Throughout your childhoods you strove to make sense of life; however you were told that life had no point or purpose and you were filled with fear. In school you had to memorize data that did not link up to anything, reinforcing the ancient limited thinking of separateness. Everything was separate, nothing was significant, everything was an accident. Most of your ancestors were encoded with this idea, yet there were always renegades. You are the renegades today, as there were renegades two thousand years ago and two thousand years before them. There are always those who do not buy the stories in the history books. Remember, the victors write the books; however those who live their own truths record their stories in their genes and in the ethers.

One of the most transformative forces in your world is feminine energy, recognized as the Mother and Goddess, which is deeply associated with love. The feminine principle brings life into being and has been the nurturing force on your globe for a long time, and the Goddess will take her place as a rightful steward of human consciousness once again. Today your world lacks an understanding of the goddess energy, which is a reflection of the lack of power of women and the lack of value that men and women have for women. A woman is the bringer of life; it is through her birthing experience—building life from egg and sperm—that the voices of the ancestors echo down through time and are imprinted into the cells of the child.

To the old pagan worshipers the goddess energy was quite prevalent in the days of enlightenment two thousand years ago. They still maintained a goddess-focused culture although it was receding more and more from the consciousness of humankind. The goddess culture understood abstract thinking; personal cycles, experiences, and their views of time were cyclical rather than linear. The demise of goddess knowledge and the rise in power of the male vibration in these last two thousand years are what led to linear thinking, reinforcing the concept "that nothing is really connected." The goddess culture understood the power of birth, that everything is alive and significant: plants, animals, and the elements of earth, air, fire, water, and ether. The people understood that the invisible ether was filled with spirits and with energy.

Your eyes are not trained to perceive the ether. A long time ago your genetic structure was set a certain way, and your biology was arranged so that you would conform to prescribed patterns of behavior. This story goes back to ancient times. You can be telepathically influenced, and energies from your creators can be sent to you as frequencies that literally rearrange your DNA. You were experimented with hundreds of thousands of years ago. Eventually you will ask, "Who are these creators?" And we will get to that part of the tale, eventually. We remind you that the story we tell is one you unfold in yourselves as it also unfolds in many cycles of time.

Those who lived close to the Earth and understood the feminine principle believed that God was in all things. They did not have one God because they were abstract thinkers. Living close to the Earth, they understood the plants and animals. Their cycles of time were marked by the solstices and the equinoxes because they took note of the heavens. They did not have newspapers; they read the world as they lived their lives. Life was more challenging, yet simpler in many ways, and people did not strive as much for the accumulation of material goods. They lived in communities and clustered together because they needed one another. Family lines were remembered and oral history was very important, so people's minds were quite sharp. They would memorize stories and trace their family lines back in time. Storytelling around a fire was often the most common form of entertainment. Holidays and ceremonies were organized around the movement of the heavens, and the modulation of light and dark ruled the old world as you know it.

The people of long ago noticed what was occurring in the heavens. They often slept outside during the summers. Huts, castles, and fortresses were used for colder weather. The sky and the atmosphere impulsed and intrigued them, and for as long as they could remember, the stories passed down to them, whether from glyphs carved in stone or from scripts and parchments, always pointed to the heavens. It seems that from the beginning of humankind the importance of the heavens was recorded in your stories. Ancient manuscripts were full of reports on what came from the heavens, and the movement and action of the heavens. Remember, no one traveled very much or knew what was happening far away from them. The big entertainment every night was in the sky. Those who could translate the activities in the sky acted as intermediaries between the stellar parents and the human constituency.

Knowledge that connected your ancestors to the Earth was very very important to them, and combined with Family of Light and their accelerated abilities to heal and teach about the frequency of love, the times were quite dynamic. Of course this knowledge would set the people free, yet many were afraid of their power and filled themselves with the vibration of fear. The authority at the time—the Old World Order, the Roman Empire—sought out the Family of Light and killed them. There were many opposing factions at the beginning of Christianity. No one could quite agree on what was what, and diametrically opposed ideas were taught because there were many teachers, not just one teacher. Today you have many teachers, yet some of you still look for only one. We see you will all have to claim your power to teach.

Now two thousand years later you are a product of the fear stored in your cells, a fear of opening to a new age of being and of being all-powerful. Your ancestors were afraid of the gladiators, of being tortured and crucified. Those who claimed their own beliefs faced these horrors. Your history is filled with fights in all countries, in all corners of the world, over whose God is God, whose beliefs are correct, who are the infidels and who are the righteous ones. Now if you look at this story from a larger perspective, you will begin to get suspicious. How could the same pattern be so predominant all over the world? Why do we find people always fighting each other over their truth, over their God, a God supposedly based on love, but a love located outside the self? Your great solution, no matter what is occurring, is to love yourself and vibrate that frequency outside yourself. Doing so will allow many doors to open, and likewise many unwanted probabilities will simply pass you by, like a bird on the wing.

Today you are faced with a recurring opportunity. Imprinted in the consciousness of humankind are the experiences of *all* of your ancestors. When the ages shift, a great opportunity is at hand, so what will you do about it? Will you claim your power? Will you claim what is in your genes? If you reach further back in your mind, you might remember another calendar point, a time exactly opposite this one in the great precession of the equinoxes: the twenty-six-thousand-year cycle or rotation of the zodiac constellations overhead. Exactly opposite your Now, about thirteen thousand years ago on the precession calendar, another important time of enlightenment occurred. It was a time when power was to be understood, a time that you yourselves remember as the final collapse of a very old civilization, a royal age unable to manifest because it was based on selfishness. No one in Atlantis counted love as the most important value. Contemplate what their experience, thirteen thousand years ago, suggests to you. What memories echo from the Atlantean hallways? The Atlantean culture reached everywhere. They were savvy with their technological skills, and they too understood the ether as an invisible spirit world, a world to travel into and to bring energies from. They understood the power of crystals and the power of the mind. More than that, they understood mind control, for the ability to control another human's mind reaches deep into time. You seem to have developed your own perfections of it in late-twentieth-century Earth; however this practice dates back into the early annals of existence, as some already know and remember.

Your tests today as human beings are not simply about meeting third-dimensional challenges, although there will be many. Your opportunity lies in understanding that in the cycles of existence, you relive points in time to reach for and achieve something unique. It is time for you to acknowledge your powers and live in the Now. Live for freedom, for the amount of freedom you have will depend upon your response-ability. If you cannot respond, then you will lock yourself into a cocoon, a web so tangled you will never wiggle out. As Family of Light, we address you: Look to what is inside yourself. The history of your world shows that people have been penalized for free thinking. You live in a world that at one time sold you a "truth": "The Earth is the center of the universe. And anyone who disagrees will be burned at the stake!"

Today you face the same shift in perception. Will you expand your vision beyond what you think and have the courage to speak and live your truth? Love from inside is essential to achieve this shift. Living begins to make sense when you realize you chose to be who you are. You are multidimensional beings, and there are many "you's" to get to know. There are versions of "you's" from a few thousand years ago and thirteen thousand years ago, who have jumped

into t   .e. And if you find you did
not l   your mind has traveled to
the   :hing exists at once, a place
wh   s on the screen of your mind,
sho   een so you can make sense of
w

i   ffling. You may feel that there
                onder: How can I make sense
                ou must. You are here to chart
                er an unnamed opportunity. By
                ver one of your greatest abilities:
                not victims. You are not flawed.
                s. And no one needs to save you.
                ze anything from books. You must
                our will and your intent to discover
                ossoming of life that is occurring in

                ted for separation, for meaningless
                eavens, and hells, it is a wonder any-
                ny more. However, love is here in a
                nat you can ever experience any place
                stiny is to turn the whole world into a
                e are here to assist you in that process.
                u. Actually, all we can really do is enter-
                leas, and perhaps act as instigators. You
                , creators, and doers. As you learn more
                and its many levels of influence, you will
                sily controlled because you do not want to
be in   ourselves. You like it when ideas come to
you, and you do not have to think. You like to be told what to
do. You surf the Internet and have no idea that the ideas you
are fed lock you in limited thinking. You do not realize your
genes can be rearranged telepathically. It is not so easy to do;
however it is done, particularly at the beginning of one age
and the end of another.

The wave of energy that comes from space to awaken you brings power. However, if you continue to give up your power to others, you will live in the greatest tyranny this world can hold, a tyranny that reaches far and eventually colonizes space. This tyranny is a secret. It exists today with the secret colonization of space, yet you are unaware of it because you are being fed a story that is only part of the truth. Space is colonized and people from your planet have been out there for a long time—on the Moon, Mars, and beyond. The planets, like you, are alive; they are electromagnetic beings that influence you, and during this time you must awaken again to the importance of the heavens.

A dark shroud has been cast over your consciousness, a darkness so vast that now so many of you are truly frightened to live. Your bodies are filled today with cancer, stress, and pollution because you have been primed for fear over the years and have drawn to yourself negative energies from the other realms, and these spirits of lower energies feed off your fear. Reality mirrors itself. The marketing of fear has been massive: Through meaningless data and meaningless living, you have drawn to yourself those who suck your power, vampires and parasites completely invisible to your perceptual acuities. They are, nonetheless, sucking your vitality because you do not want to claim it. We will say to you, dear humans, love yourselves, place value on who you are. As you move forward and understand the unfolding absurdity of your times and why your civilization is collapsing, love yourselves. As you shift your perceptions, you will be able to rebuild your civilization based on value and respect for all life, including your multidimensional ancestors, your multidimensional parents, and your reincarnational selves. As a diamond your facets include all of them, as you discover who you are.

A healing is at hand, although at first it will appear as if your world has been rent asunder. Only in the shattering can the rebuilding occur. Our words convey an energy that will carry you into the twenty-first century, creating a bridge of sorts, a bridge built in your minds, and one based on truth. Only you will figure out what truth is for yourselves. Remember, whatever truth you choose, it shall be. Family of Light said two thousand years ago, "As you think, so shall it be. Do unto others as you would have them do unto you." This teaching comes around again; this time when Family of Light returns will you go before the gladiators? Or will you splinter and fracture and fight among yourselves? Will you argue over who is who and what is what? You could look yourselves up in your old cellular files and say, "Ah, we have been here before, we have seen that last time we blew a great opportunity. We created fear and pain and two thousand years of separation for humankind. And all of the greatness of the time was missed."

Be uplifted at this go-around; for one more time, you get to do it again! We ask you, please, do it with valor and humor. Meet everything you create with courage. Think of your ancestors, of your bloodline and the limitation put upon it. Then think about the light that you are, as well as your ancestors' light, for in some way there has always been a spirit that kept people going. Imagine yourselves removed from everyday living and looking at Earth across time. Can you see the foibles and follies of humankind, as well as the victories? If you as students of Earth were to list the victories of humanity, what would they be? And if you were to list the victories of your own lives, what would they be? See if you can come up with a few. We will tell you that the true victories will always involve the vibration of love. All the knowledge in the universe cannot equal the frequency of love.

Even though you are connected to a whole that whole is separated into many parts, and those parts are vibrating now with difficulty because they are separated. Often those parts want to be separated because it makes them feel more powerful. This is the dilemma Family of Light faces. How do you share power with everyone? Why does it appear that one branch, called Family of Dark, has accrued more power than Family of Light? Why does Family of Light sometimes feel like victims? Why does Family of Dark have money, wealth, prestige, the interdimensional connections, and the secrets?

You know that a few people rule your world and have done so for a long long time. The few over the many. As we mentioned, the Gods came here eons ago and mated with humans; they stopped off here, stayed a few hundred years, and were gone. They started the lineage of blue blood, which indicates a stellar link to the heavens. Because everything is transferred from ancestor to ancestor, those who track their bloodlines and claim celestial lineage are very careful to keep themselves together. In general they do not spread their vibration or ancestral seed to those they control. They form a select group, a cabal, and rule your world in secret. You know some of them, others you do not. When the Gods came, they left a hierarchy of presidents and popes, kings and queens, princes and princesses and patriarchs. There are those who are very knowledgeable about planetary history, and they do indeed understand that another form of intelligence has been communicating with your world for eons. They keep that knowledge to themselves because they have been so instructed.

The Gods have not really gone away; they have simply taken a nap. Time is different for them so it appears that the Gods have forgotten you, but they have not. They are here, and this is why you must awaken. You must ask: Who are the Gods? Who are these invisible forces? Who is Family of Light? Who is Family of Dark? Who are the Gods of Family of Dark? Who are the Gods of Family of Light? Who are the Goddesses of everyone? And who am *I* in this process?

The Game of Life

As we look at the Book of Earth and turn its pages, we see many things. Because we exist outside of your time, we see what has slipped between the cracks and what was not put in your history books, which by the way barely hold a thread of the great tapestry of your rich and varied history. You may be wondering at this point what kind of book could we interdimensional travelers be viewing. We call it a book because you believe that you learn from books. One of the questions we would now like to ask is this: How have you arrived at your thinking? Where do your ideas and knowledge come from, and why do you credit some knowledge and discredit others?

Open your mind as you read our words for we speak to the library of knowledge inside of you. It is the same library of knowledge that we call the Book of Earth, a rich and varied texture of living history. One of the great issues you face today is how to identify yourself. Will you believe everything that you read in your books and newspapers and view on your videos, movies, and Internet? Are these the reference guides for your beliefs? In the Book of Earth there are ways to understand who you are. You were designed with purpose and move through the heavens on a synchronized journey, one set into motion by beings whose intelligence you cannot begin to grasp. When we have sought to understand ourselves and why we think what we think, even we have encountered forces of existence so gigantic that we pale in comparison. These Builders of Universes are not vague, nebulous beings; they are composite intelligences, unified in their understanding of the universal energies. They create extensions of their knowledge, bringing their knowledge into form, and call you part of that knowledge of Earth. And you use or do not use the power of your mind to structure this "knowledge."

As you may know, energy precedes matter and form, and here on Earth your thoughts and perceptions transfer energy into form. So when we speak about calendars of time, they are convenient creations through which you can locate meanings in reality. Your mind likes divisions; therefore you name and label and place things in order. Your ancestors, however, had a different way of using their minds; they were far more in tune with the larger cycles of living. You live through a sequence of decades, and every time you shift a decade it is a big deal. Your ancestors used a different counting of time. Rather than locating themselves precisely in time, they perceived time outside themselves. They lived precisely in the moment, in the Now, for time was rich for them in the Now, and there time opened the pages of Earth, the pages of their ancestors, the pages of living. What they chose to think and believe often came from oral tradition, the exchanging of stories, living close to the land, and through deep telepathic connection and an astute awareness. A need-to-know basis created their abilities. Today you live in a world where you do not want to know, let alone *need* to know what is happening around you. You have abdicated the power of thinking and do not even know how thinking arose. Consider that everyone who has ever lived on Earth continues to move forward and affect their genetic line. Generations of blood and knowledge have been passed down from one human to another. Everything every human has ever experienced is recorded in the great being of your biological structure you call the human body, which, again, is greater than any computer you could ever design.

As we have said, you are not capable, in all truth, of designing a machine greater than yourself. Everything you design is a mirror reflection of your own greatness, and it pays to understand that. As our story unfolds, we will look through the Book of your planetary tales to see where other civilizations and forms of intelligence faced the same series of lessons. We will look at the path that they chose and what it taught them. Perhaps in our tales and calling forth of your cellular memory, you will know it all by the end. That is our intent. How you think and communicate is how you know yourself and how you arrive at your beliefs about yourself. Clear communication is the essence of understanding. Your ancestors, whether they lived ten years or twelve thousand years ago, had different modes of communication and yet the results were similar. Whoever had the loudest voice created the belief system. The history of your world is filled with the voice of the victor, the voice of power, although it was not always a voice of sanity by any means. The so-called victors often knew about the secrets hidden in the mysteries of Earth and her people, secrets passed down from antiquity. What kind of secrets could your ancestors have known? We will begin to tell you; however you must stretch your consciousness as well to reach for this understanding.

Secrets were stored in the hidden stories of Earth and in your blood. You have incarnated and experienced Earth and her records many times; her Library, her Book, is even imprinted in the atmosphere. The very atmosphere that sustains you is a form of energy and intelligence, used for communication because it can store information. Actually, everything around you is energy holding the story of what you are, and you keep exchanging that energy with your molecules. Every time you exhale you are giving off a part of yourself, and when you inhale you add something more. You live within a visual agreement where, as solid beings, you faithfully replicate the same scenarios again and again. Basically you do not question whether or not there is another way of thinking and being. You are used to a linear, defined, and expected experience; therefore, you create it.

Your ancestors thought of time as part of a large cycle called the precession of the equinoxes, caused by the wobble of your planet on its axis, which makes the constellations of the zodiac appear to move across the heavens in a 26,000-year cycle. Who lives long enough to count time in this way? you may ask. Well, that is a good question. You may have to expand your thinking to perceive that at one time human beings lived on Earth much longer than you currently do. Three hundred-year or even, at one time, 10,000-year age spans were not so uncommon. And a long time ago in the Books of Important People, there were those who lived for a few hundred thousand years. How could that be? you ask. Or why would they want to? We will come to that. For now just imagine that it is possible.

The cycle of time that is counted again and again in the Book of Earth is this 26,000-year period, which is the amount of time, in your terms, for the twelve constellations of the zodiac to complete one cycle of movement across the heavens. This grand cycle of time creates one Great Year and contains the various ages delineated by the signs of the zodiac. Through the marking of time, you can begin to discern patterns, and patterns indicate order and purpose. In a quiet moment imagine there is a purpose to being. Everything is designed and planned in an impeccable, synchronistic order, and you are involved in it; you are not purposeless little molecules struggling in a meaningless world; you are part of the significant plan, which can be seen from many different angles. The greatest of covert operators may discredit the idea of an immense plan because, no matter how finely they are tuned, they cannot conceive of a greater energy that designs existence. Likewise, many people cannot conceive of this immense order because they lack the intent of love or goodwill at the core of their beings. The universe and all you experience are inherently built on love, a love so grand that it allows evil its own reign, knowing that even within evil there is a purpose. A purpose exists in all things, though there is never just one purpose just as there is never one history, one calendar, or one way of interpreting anything. There are many ways of seeing.

We ask you to imagine the Book of Earth and to begin to delineate the ages in your mind. Imagine this 26,000-year cycle divided into twelve sections, each one almost twenty-two hundred years long. The era called the millennium at the year 2000 is based upon an agreement. Many will argue and say the third millennium date is inaccurate and this is true. However the date is based on a long-standing agreement, and agreements create reality. The creation of time is an agreement, and the heavens comply, assisting you to use time to locate yourselves in existence. Now locate yourselves in the moment by noticing your breath, and then imagine you have lived many times, or imagine your ancestors who lived before you. Earth has been populated throughout the various ages, and each age has a theme, a purpose to achieve. The twelve ages have seasons just like your 365-day year, and each age can be divided into four, approximately 500- to 550-year slices of time where lessons are to be learned. If you were to reincarnate quickly, you would have a number of lifetimes in each 500-year period.

Currently you are at the end of the Piscean Age, one of twelve slices of time rippling with richness and purpose. You are entering the Age of Aquarius, which heralds an awakening and unifying of humanity. The closing doors of the

Piscean Age bring forth themes of compassion and enlightenment through complete connection with the universal mind.
Interesting situations occur during these times, conveying the
lessons of your ancestors: Their challenges, victories, and
daily living experiences all resonate through time into you. As
you expand your view of time, remember that knowledge is
passed through the bloodline, whether a "blue" blood or a
"red" blood. The biology of your being is rich, yet as with
using a computer, you must know how to access what is there.
Genetically, so much is within you that beings in the heavens
have managed you for eons so that you would not be connected to all that you are. They reap their harvest from your
ignorance, through your willingness to give up the power of
thinking, to eagerly obey, to be on time, to die, and basically
to accept being told what to do. The story we unfold makes
sense when you understand why you have come here, how
long the lessons have been accruing, and where you are in this
season of growth.

Movement through the ages shifts the lessons of the current civilization, bringing about the opportunities necessary
for gathering experiences essential to their purpose. Each age
has its high and low points. There is really no point in con-
demning one civilization and acknowledging another, because each existed for a distinct purpose. Certainly reaching
the end of one age and the beginning of another is momentous; therefore it is essential for you to understand what you
face. Imagine that you can hear the tales of your ancestors as
if they were alive and gathered around a fire, speaking to you
of their journeys and adventures. If you remember this feeling
in the quiet moments of daily living and feel these people rich
and alive, you will know you are tapping into your own Book
of Earth. We use this description to capture an image, and you
can use it as well, though in actuality the stories are in the
ethers, for the atmosphere itself holds the records of energy.
Our intention is to teach you how to read these molecules of

intelligence, to discover inside yourself which buttons to push, which programs to access, and the way in which to activate your brilliant biological form.

Now imagine the twelve ages, each with its own lesson. At the beginning and the end of each age, there is always an acceleration of energy that acts as a bridge between the last two hundred or so years of a 2200-year age and a few hundred years into the next. Each age has a destiny to experience, a spiritual weather so to speak. There are ages with new beginnings and ages of great blossomings as well as ages of harvest. And then there are the ages you call winter, the ages of building spiritual conclusions where one retreats deep inside to access the entire purpose of the experiments in living.

As human beings you enter Earth at birth and interact with living through your family. You are drawn for many reasons to the people of your bloodline. Sometimes you have lived with them before in a direct kin relationship; other times you follow souls you are deeply connected to and move from one bloodline to another. If you were able to trace your ancestral tree back for thousands of years, you would find that as an individual you chose to pop in and out of your own bloodline. Today you are often assessed, especially by those in power, by the quality of the blood that runs in your veins.

One of the biggest secrets to understanding how you have arrived at your thinking process involves knowing that Heavenly Beings exist beyond the slices of time in which you live, and that periodically they visit you. Humans are considered to be a part of certain celestial principalities, a biological experiment available for study. As we said, we refer to your world as Library of Earth, a place where beings are created genetically in the likeness of what you call God, and then set about to live within lessons and seasons of time that are influenced by energy. Where does the influencing energy come from? Actually this energy is gathered from your movement through the heavens, as well as from the sun. Think about this: What would you do without the sun? Where would you get your food? Where would you get your ideas? Ideas are indeed transmitted on light. The modulation between light and dark and the precision with which they are rendered to your consciousness determine how you perceive reality. This concept is key to understanding how systems of consciousness are designed, and how universes and galaxies and solar systems are put into place. You design games about your reality, then sell them in stores, and play them for entertainment. Actually, beings much grander than you or we are—the intelligence behind synchronized, meaningful living—create realities in that same way. Within their great blueprint of the game of life, there is always a plan. Today intelligent waves of light energy designed as seasons of psychic weather hit Earth in an unpredictable way, all part of a plan.

The ruling families of Earth have always kept track of their bloodline and have continued to decode their connection to the celestials who seeded them eons ago. Sometimes they understand their own reincarnational existences; however part of their mistake has been to remain within their own particular bloodline, which then becomes bloated, electrically discharged, and devoid of light, managing much power but with no purpose. This power seeks to hoard energy, treasures, and ultimately knowledge of existence. These bloodliners are connected to a vast invisible energy that barely any human can understand. Members of the twelve or thirteen families that rule your world have a deep and secret understanding of the division of the twelve ages of the Great Year. In actuality they know that at one time the ages were divided into thirteen and that by changing the way time is interpreted, slices of knowledge and experience have been cut out.

How you think is the focus in this lesson. You believe you learned what you know in school, or perhaps you read the newspaper every day. Your mother and father, forms of government, and religious organizations all affect you, but how will you reach beyond the knowledge and information passed to you that define your world? Your ancestors managed this because they used time differently. When we speak of the Book that allows us to look through time, our intent is to contort the way in which you view time so that as you rebuild an image of time in your mind, you will have a new codex for exploring experiences encoded in time in the cells of your being.

Now, each age had celestial contact, and sometimes the contact was widely acknowledged and understood, considered to be an important part of the belief system of the current civilization. Each age had a way of dealing with the realm of the supernatural. If you trace history in your mind to A.D. 0, you will find that your calendar counting punctuates its beginning with the arrival of the being you call Christ. Energy points at the shifting of the ages create tremendous activity, and Family of Light, who likes to bring in and bridge information, often arrives with their own agendas to teach. Each civilization, in its age, has the opportunity to exalt or to destroy itself. By choosing to be exalted, an ongoing impetus is created, teaching laws of existence that had been lost. Through destruction there is nothing left. In the Book of Earth, your world exists for billions of years. The cycle of time we ask you to consider, twenty-six thousand years, is but a small speck. Many a civilization has developed and flourished for a long long time, and then has destroyed itself. If you existed forever in one form, who would you be?

In your third-dimensional world, it may always appear that you destroy yourselves, one civilization after another; however, in the Book of Earth, any civilization can be visited and located if one knows the coordinates and uses the proper frequency. You are just learning these techniques on Earth at this time. Using technology, the manipulation and bending of time have been secretly practiced for almost the past one hundred years; although for thousands of years, even without technology, time-jumping has occurred. Those who read the mysteries and understood the hidden secrets always knew how to move through time. Sometimes only visions appeared; at other times relocation was possible, and sometimes people vanished because they slipped into another aspect of time. You do not need technology or time machines to time-travel, although today governments of the world do experiment with this technology behind your back.

Much of the chaos happening in late-twentieth-century Earth is the result of a massive shift caused by time-jumpers, moving in and out of your time looking for particular events or wanting to change probable worlds. Worlds can be changed. The Book of Earth can be changed. One can go backward and forward in time because everything is significant and alive and everything affects everything else. You may wonder how there can be a Book of Earth if it is always changing. How can there even be history if the Book of Earth, the Book of Time, can change? Well, how fixed is what you believe to be true? How fixed is the Civil War, or World War I, or Babylon, or Nebuchadnezzar's dream?

As the constellations pass overhead on what is called the zodiacal belt, you encounter different energies. Whenever an age shifts, one of the unique opportunities is for Earth to transmit rather than receive energy frequencies. Those coming to Earth now are jumping time and entering because they know a vast change will soon occur on how you use energy. Everyone is fighting for control, anxious to see who will win. Will you as humans step gracefully into your power, understanding the great lessons the Book of Earth embodies? We come through time to share the lessons we have learned: that reality mirrors itself, that war creates war, that love creates love, that withholding energies for power creates separation and separation creates illness. You cannot be separated from the whole, so in some way you must unite. All shifts of ages have to create a bridge of energy, sharing the accumulation of one age with the next. Benchmark points of the ages are punctuated by peak or primary events. Because you are at the end of an age, perhaps you are wondering what the primary event will be?

You are in the process of building a wave of revolutionary energy in relationship to your mind and how you think. Two thousand years ago Family of Light taught an energy of truth and love and brought forth the message, "As you think so shall it be." The records of Family of Light were later compiled, rearranged, and portrayed as the life of a single character: Jesus Christ. You do not have a clear, precise picture in your history books of who lived at that time. People of great power walked the land and taught the truth of the vibration of love; as well, they helped people recognize the tyranny they lived under. Tyranny uses the tool of fear to control you. One of the ongoing tests you face from one age to another, from one season to another, and truly from one moment to the next, is understanding fear. When you buy into any version of fear, it can become your experience because your molecules are intelligent and your energy responds to the predominant feeling in your being. The focus of your mind is exactly what gives the orders to create what you experience. Even though your ancestors approached reality from a different point of view, they too had to pass the test of fear, just as you shall in the days ahead.

Your ancestors also utilized the body in a very different way from you because they used the whole brain. As you may know the right side of your brain is connected with the left side of the body, and it is the basis of an unbounded energy of intuition and creativity. The left side of your brain, which is the side most employed during the last two thousand years, is slowly being developed for logic. Two thousand years ago marked the end of cyclical living. Over the next few hundred years, into the beginning of the Piscean Age, there were those who still lived by cycles and talked with the Gods and understood the Gods as friendly, and often kind beings. They had retained their beliefs from the preceding Age of Aries, dominated by big empires which strove to capture the Gods in form by creating elaborate statuary and building large architectural structures in tribute to these beings. These people were versed in abstract thinking as well as understanding its linear components. They also understood the energy the Egyptians embodied in the idea of the Ka, the spirit that speaks to you as a double, the other self. When the knowledge of cyclical living began to change, people lost touch with the significance of life. They forgot about the spiritual seasons and that life has purpose. The bridge into the first century involved living the truth of love. There was a great great battle for truth then, just as there is today. Whose truth would it be?

The Roman Empire was the ruling order of the day; its purpose was the unification of two powerful forces: the management of spirit and the governing of existence. In order to truly grasp an understanding of your history and your thinking process, you must factor in the invisibles and consider what the goddess and pagan cultures understood: The so-called Gods are many and have had many names. The Christian Church, incorporated into the Roman Empire, began its tyranny of your minds by doling out spiritual truths, and those in authority then began to change history by rewriting the books. The Gods were renamed and their activities, devoid of benefits, were given attributes of Satan, fear, and evil. The new thoughtform, supposedly based on love, was in actuality an energy designed to control you, and once again you gave your power to think over to a new authority, and fear became more dominant than love. This has happened to each of you over and over again. You forget to love.

The management of minds became dominant in order to rule the souls, spirits, and energies of the people, and a shift occurred from whole-brain thinking, which valued intellect and intuition, to intellectual thinking only. In the last two thousand years, you have slowly and completely given away your power, first by allowing others to tell you what to think, and secondly by accepting the dictate that your connection to spirit could only be maintained through an organization, an intermediary. Religious ideas became compromises of spiritual knowledge and were appropriated by the state. Local Pagans, keepers of the seasons and the cycles, keepers of whole knowledge and the Goddess, were compromised.

Two thousand years ago when the modern-day management of minds began, a great opportunity for love existed. There has always been an invisible frequency battle for the influence of how the experiment of humans will be conducted and conveyed, because there are those who live off the frequencies you produce. What are these frequencies? you may ask. Everything you do, in every moment of your life, produces a frequency. Now think about this, and then feel it. *Everything you do in every moment of your life produces a frequency.* Why? Because you are a biological being designed to be a frequency generator and your emotions are the tuning key. You have feelings about everything whether you want to admit them or not. Even though many of you never express your feelings, they still exist in a cumulative pattern, stored in the cells of your being and in your blood, just as they have in the lives of all your ancestors. The patterns radiate out from you in electromagnetic waves that have signals that call to you what you put out.

You are connected to something bigger than yourself. From the beginning of time, men and women have spoken with the spirits because the Gods were friendly and have always been around. It is only recently that the Gods have been managed and kept from you. At the beginning of the Piscean Age, it was decreed that only certain people could talk to God, that God was not available for everyone except through offerings of money, through prayers, and through priests and popes. A Dark Age then came over the land, an age of sickness, of ignorance, and of great fear. The second 500-year period in this 2,000-year test of time was very dark.

However, whenever there is dark, there is also light. And as the light dawned, many people began to awaken. At the beginning of the Middle Ages, from A.D. 1000 to approximately A.D. 1500, new ideas were brought forth. An awakening of human consciousness was occurring once again. However, before this new freedom of thought could take hold, there was a last eruption of darkness, the Inquisition, which was filled with killing and destruction. It was initiated by those who wanted to control the abode of the Deity and how it could be reached; they also wanted to limit people's thinking. If you did not think according to what was correct, you were taken in the night and killed. There were fewer people then so it was easier to manage them. Your ancestors lived with the fear of knowing secrets and of breaking the rules for what was officially permitted. There were very few who would stand forward and say, "Ah ha, the Emperor is naked, he wears no clothes." Fear was so great in frequency around the Earth that, whenever someone did speak out, everyone else moved into fear instead of love. A lesson for living in your time will be similar. When truthsayers have the courage to say the emperor is wearing no clothes, whether you agree with their point of view or not, send them love. They are to be acknowledged for speaking their truth.

It is important to speak your truth, not to convince anyone else of it. Everyone must make up their own minds. Please remember, one of the great lessons you are learning, as we see it in the Book of Earth, is to realize you have given over the power of thinking and have forgotten how to think for yourselves. You live now in boxes and follow calendars and think the moment that was once before you is forever gone, and you erase yourselves as you move faster and faster into a future of purposeless living. Family of Light knows that humankind is immersed in a race toward change, an experiment you must all participate in by changing yourselves. For those of you who are open to ideas and who can hear the message we convey, remember it is not necessary to convert or preach. Simply know in the core of your beings that you are all riding the arriving wave of change. Do your best to keep your wits about you, make your own decisions, know what you want, keep yourselves open to the great mysteries, and know that no matter how much you know, it is still only a few pages in the great Book of Existence.

We see that late-twentieth-century Earth is a destiny point, and there is a sense of urgency that we and many others feel about this location in time. From your point of view, the point expands across what you would call "many years." As we view your world, we see a short period of time, actually encapsulated in about twenty-five of your years—from 1987 to 2012—that passes like a nanosecond and is hardly detectable in the vastness of All That Is. Of course it is easy to jump to Babylon—it existed for ages. Many other cultures, kingdoms, and civilizations had greater longevity, not here one moment and gone the next. You however are living in a time when everything is fragmented, separated, and unconnected, when the winds of time are wispy and the fibers are not so thick.

There were fewer civilizations and thought systems in your ancestors' days, fewer bloodlines and fewer purposes. The experiment was more controlled. Certainly the experiment was always focused on the area called the Middle East, known as the Fertile Crescent, which is filled with ancient structures. The pyramids located in Egypt were used as sound devices to communicate with the heavens. They were also used as weights to balance electromagnetic forces and actually to create an acupuncture point of energy into the Earth grid. The Great Pyramid does not exist above the ground only: Below ground the structure pierces the earth so cosmic energy can be transmitted and grounded from one age to another. The Great Pyramid, as you presently know it, has been around for a long long time. Records and stories from your modern historians need of course to be reconsidered. All of the ancient structures built in stone had a celestial influence, and are far more ancient and have greater purpose than your history books tell you.

As you consider the knowledge we share with you, perhaps you find yourselves undertaking tasks that do not always make sense. You may seek to track down your roots by visiting sacred sites, or perhaps Egypt has called many of you back to its corridors. You would actually be called to the corridors of the old Persian Empire, the area of Iran and Iraq, if you could get in. Over the last few decades, great trouble has been brewing there to keep you from entering. It is a key area in the development of human consciousness as part of the Fertile Crescent where the Gods played their games and implemented their experiments. You are still being watched to see how you will create your reality. Will you destroy yourselves, will you create a new world, what will you figure out? Will you look outside the parameters of your finely tuned perceptions or will you live in a bubble of ignorance, believing everything that is told to you? You are observed and studied over time. And because you reincarnate again and again, you propagate yourselves and eventually you trap yourselves in this process.

There are beings who observe you to whom twenty-six thousand years is one year in your terms. One year. See if you can imagine those who are grander than yourselves, beings who watch you, who meddle with and influence you in order to understand and learn from you. When you think of twenty-six thousand years being one year in their experience, what then is the twenty-five-year period we speak of, starting in late-twentieth-century Earth? How can they find it? How do we find it? To you it may seem as if twenty-five years is a long time; to many it is merely a blink of an eye. According to the Book of Earth, as we scan the pages backward and forward to understand you and ourselves, that twenty-five-year period is a significator. It is unique because it has more threads of time and probabilities running into it than any other time anywhere in existence.

We have asked you to consider how you arrive at your thinking. Certainly by now you may already be questioning what you learned in school, what has been purported as important to know. Your challenge is to reexplore history as you know it and to look at life from a larger point of view. Use the cells of your being, the sounds of living, and Earth herself to stimulate you. Step outside of the abode of the Deity that tells you what to think and step into the abode of yourselves. Learn how to think and then decide what you want to believe. This takes courage; however you are not alone. The bridge from one age to another is always bustling with tremendous activity. As electromagnetic energies change, the Earth's magnetic field is becoming weaker; physical and mental structures are not held in place in the same way. When the magnetic field weakens, chaos occurs.

How you handle chaos is another major test. What you do as reality is scrambled will determine your ongoing experience. One of the great reasons why you, as Family of Light, are here is to experience living from your own point of view. Your new interpretation of existence, running through every cell of your being, will be transmitted from your auric field and affect the living biological sphere of Earth. Ideally you will transmit a new frequency into existence.

At the end of an age, an accumulation of knowledge is transmitted. So what will you transmit? We asked you earlier what would you count as your victories? Imagine that you make contact with beings who dwell beyond time. Imagine that they ask you to define yourselves and tell them what you think you know about yourselves. What would you say? What books would you give them to put in the galactic libraries, offered as your contribution? Think about it. Would it be books about the inventions from the last fifty years, or from the last decade of the century? What would be the focus of importance? Anything you come up with, we would say, limits you in some way. This exercise will help you understand where thinking came from, and why you think what you do. Then perhaps you will rethink yourselves.

Perhaps, with the aid of your ancestors, you can understand the ages of time and cycles of influence that vie for your attention and your biological energy, which you emit as emotions. Perhaps you will begin to understand that your energy is being harvested, and that others watch you from moment to moment. We said earlier that the Gods have taken a nap. That's only from your point of view. Someone is always connected and around. When you vibrate with fear, you draw energies to you of that vibration. We ask you all to consider, without guilt, shame, or blame: How much fear do you produce in the world? Now imagine that the vibration you send out, without your even thinking about it, attracts a form of life capable of influencing you, to keep you producing that same vibration. Without the fear these energies would have to leave because they do not resonate with love. In the bigger picture, in the Book of Earth as the pages unfold, we see time and time again, no matter which Empire is in charge—Persian, Roman, or Greek with the Great Alexander stepping forward to conquer the world—they are all based on fear and killing.

Today the New World Order has a chance to be another Roman Empire. The Roman Empire merged with Christianity in the early centuries of this era and modulated the truth of Family of Light to fit their political agenda. Will those of you who are bringers of truth today modulate your truth to be one with the New World Order? The ancient Christians were divided; far from being unified, they were diversified in their teachings. Some believed that there was more than one God, while others believed in only one. We say, if there is one God, it is Love. Love can personify itself in many ways. The grandness and intelligence of Love, which you call Creator, accept all things. It does not condemn what you call Gods and Goddesses for being rambunctious or for making and destroying life, because love itself, the Creator, is constantly created and destroyed. In the bigger picture, everything is imprinted with an ongoing intelligence and nothing is ever really destroyed. As you rethink yourself, think about Earth and the destruction taking place today. Your biosphere, your physical beings, your backyards, fields, and meadows are in jeopardy. The places where children used to play and run by streams, spending the afternoon under trees, studying clouds as they passed through the sky, are slowly disappearing. Once squirrels and birds were valued; now they are feared as germ-infested creatures.

Magic was once alive. With the selling of linear thinking and the erasing of the cyclical meaning of existence, magic has vanished. It vanished with the burning of the witches. They were the last brave ones to carry forth the teachings. To bring up witches may raise some hackles. There are as many versions of the witch stories as there are versions of truth. Many so-called witches were actually those who defied the ultimate tyranny of mind called religious truth. They still spoke to the land, like the ancient Pagans, and understood the herbs as medicines. They practiced natural healing remedies and knew how to live in a time of darkness. They dared to reach into the ethers, into the realm of spirits, and communicate with them. They were called "cavorters with the Devil," so they were taken from their homes, their villages, and burned publicly. A great fear spread through the land for the Inquisition had many methods of torture. However every age always has its renegades, those who quietly know how to blend in and play the game, who understand that in every moment of living there is a choice: low road, middle road, or high road. The quality of love or fear you carry into each moment determines which road you travel. Even in the darkest of times, those who understood the frequency of love knew how to shroud themselves, and so the mysteries of cyclical living were carried forth.

This was certainly not what governments or religious organizations taught. People were told they needed to be governed; that they were not capable of talking to God personally and needed intermediaries; that if they were communicating directly, they must be possessed by the Devil. The Devil's favorite subjects were women of course because women still had vestiges of the intuitive side of the brain from the pagan days. Try as they would to excise cyclical knowledge and implant linear thinking, women simply could not make the shift for many reasons. They noticed that their bleeding time was on a cycle that followed the moon as it changed and passed through its phases every twenty-eight or twenty-nine days. Their whole way of living and bringing life forth was based on cycles that contradicted the existence of a linear, meaningless world.

The removal of magic and whole living transpired during the third 500-year period of the Piscean Age, in a time approximately between A.D. 1000 and A.D. 1500. As we said, as an age unfolds, each quarter section of the age offers lessons. By the beginning of the last quarter of the Piscean Age, fear seemed to be the predominant feeling for the common person; however, in this same quarter, from A.D. 1500 to the present, the higher echelons of society experienced an enlivening of their spirit. Health and dietary practices changed, and people began to reform their old beliefs. The church and government no longer stood as ultimate authority where heretics were once burned at the stake. An Age of Enlightenment, an Age of Reason began. But what would that reason bring? Looking at the last quarter of the Piscean Age, you can see a major acceleration of information distributed among the masses. A great population explosion occurred, and people shifted from a constricted, prescribed view of a flat world to seeing the world as a globe, a world that had another side, a world that held possibilities.

Whenever new territories open, whether thousands of years ago or tomorrow in your time, many want to advertise their beliefs there. *Remember, your beliefs are based on very simple choices: fear and love.* As the New World began to be developed, the Old World Order, the Roman Empire, was already a thousand years dead and gone. The New World was discovered by European explorers but it certainly was not new. There were people here who kept the ancient stories hidden, people who dispersed during the Great Migration after the Tower of Babel. They brought with them the knowledge they held from the time of the Gods and translated it into their own words. In time their books were dispersed all over the globe. In retrospect it can be seen that it was only the Western world, a product of the Roman Empire and Christianity and a certain mode of thinking, who did not understand that the world was round. They thought it was flat because that is what they were told.

Many of the challenges of the ages resurrect themselves today in your day-to-day living. At the beginning of the last quarter point around A.D. 1500, people were challenged with accepting a worldview that instantly changed the agreed mode of living. As much as the Church wanted to burn heretics like Galileo and Copernicus who dared to challenge its ideas, they did not burn Columbus because they could not make the roundness of the world go away. Perhaps the Church and the ancient authorities could tell the people what to think about the heavens; however they could no longer promote the belief that people lived in an isolated, meaningless, fear-filled world where if you walked too far, you might fall off into the Devil's territory. Once again a bridge to freedom had the opportunity to build itself. But what was built? During this period, witches were still being burned for speaking to plants and casting spells, for basically using their will and intent to have reality meet their needs. The witches and the ancients understood many things about the body. Churches and governments wanted no knowledge about the body taught; as a result people did not bathe and wore many clothes and were terrified, and it is a wonder they reproduced.

There were always the renegades, as we have said, who did not buy the official story, but who played the game instead. They believed what they wanted to believe, and they survived. In the most toxic and volatile of times people always survive. Plagues moved over the European continent many times in the last two thousand years, decimating millions and millions of people. At times over half, maybe two-thirds of the population was wiped out. Perhaps as you consider our perspective on the Book of Earth, you will notice that you face some of the same dilemmas today.

The Fertile Crescent from Sumeria to Egypt, the Mediterranean, and Europe, were areas the Gods chose for their experiment because many different cultures could be placed in close proximity and easily monitored. Natural boundaries of mountains, deserts, and bodies of water kept the humans separated. An energy grid was opened using the Sphinx and Great Pyramid as well as many other structures that sprang up in these areas over the eons. In actuality that entire area is a doorway into your world, a doorway where the ancient ones found a space, which you can think of perhaps in terms of buying a space on the Internet, a space in virtual reality. The creation of civilizations around Sumeria and the surrounding areas was like buying a space in a virtual reality of Earth where an experiment could be seeded, a place where the Gods could put up their site and establish the commerce, business, and experience of living.

The Gods have interesting capabilities. Your ancestors were telepathically linked to them because they were whole-brained, in tune with cyclical living, and able to move energy around their bodies. At the beginning of the Piscean Age, thinking began to crystallize, solidifying the human experience, leading to greater and greater separation. Finally, during the past five hundred years, the idea arose that you are mechanized beings. Descartes and Darwin delineated a separate existence, defining life as isolated, compartmentalized, significant of itself perhaps, yet a marvel of meaningless wonder. A mass marketing of meaningless separation took hold, not only separating you from the Gods but from Nature as well, achieving the complete control of your minds. A similar story has happened all over the globe. Perhaps those in Africa can track a different time line; however their history portrays the giving away of their power to authority, giving up love, choosing war, and then losing everything. In the final isolation disease runs rampant. South America has a little different story with the same issues. There the aristocracy and the common man are vastly separated by a hierarchy with immense resources but no unification of purpose.

Secrecy and misuse of energy rule these areas today, and people are afraid to claim their power. Asia contains one of the greatest experiences of mind control ever. In the vast experiment of China, how do people think? They are told what to think. Families are allowed to have one child, and one child only. What can they do? They are one billion people, one-fifth of your planet's population. A potential grassroots movement larger than any other made complacent. How indeed have human beings been sold such limitation? When we look at the Book of Earth, we see that again and again there have been those who would speak the truth. Often they are not burned at the stake: They are laughed at.

You must begin to understand the energy at the quarter points of the last two thousand years. The lessons of an age at the quarter sections serve as punctuation points in time. Now that you are removed from those times, perhaps you can understand that you live for a purpose and that the heavens offer you energetic opportunities to become one with yourselves. Understanding this, and perhaps who you are, the history of your world then begins to make more sense.

We again remind you to rethink yourself, and to use the power of your mind to access the richness of your ancestors and your inheritance. Look around to see what you have created and know that it means more than you attribute to it. The bridge to the twenty-first century will be built in your mind. The questions are: Whose mind is it? Who owns your mind? Who battles for your mind? How veiled is the control for thinking? Contemplate these ideas as we explore more of the family secrets, the secrets inside the self, the secret miracles the body will perform using the power of the will, as we unlock the secrets of blood, sexuality, healing, creating, and living. Living is being and being is knowing that you are connected. It is this that you carry over the bridge, the idea that you live in a purposeful, a significant, and a connected world.

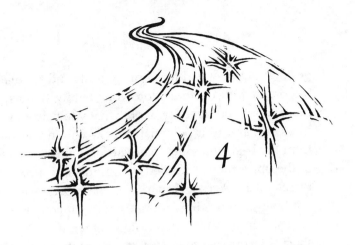

4

Your Great Inheritance

When we speak to you about this great Book of Earth, we want you to understand that the source of these stories, which are alive and rich, is stored in the annals of your genes, if only you could read them. So do not feel that we have access to knowledge that will forever be kept from you. Everything you want to know can be discovered if only you will learn to utilize the great biological being that you are.

Now that you have been reading our stories and tales of your history, you may have noticed that we jump around and say a little bit here and a little bit there. This is done so you will not think of your past unfolding in a linear line. We want you to discover who you have been and who your ancestors are in a different way, a way that may appear to be random and scattered.

When we look at the Book of Earth, we see the key juncture points where bridges are always built during the shifting of the ages. You are at one of these points, and it is by understanding your physical being, your biological structure, that you too will be able to access the same vistas and points of view that we have. We have pointed to your ancestors, suggesting that they had faced many trials and tribulations. It is important for you to explore your family tree as you learn more about your identity, about what you value and who you think you are. Your potential to grow within yourself is taken from the basic founding materials of your true ancestry. Part of the opportunity afforded you in the shift from the Age of Pisces to the Age of Aquarius is the movement from linear thinking to multidimensional living. If you were instantaneously thrust from one era to another, it would be quite a shock to your nervous system; yet within the bloodline of your ancestral lineage is the ability to shift your reality by shifting your perceptions.

In late-twentieth-century Earth, you are rediscovering psychic phenomena, the psi factor as you call it, which the Pagans and Witches knew as Spirit or Ether. Religious leaders, who organized and sold their version of God to you, have always maintained that psychic powers were of the Devil because they did not want people to acquire this power. Over time your ancestors chose fear and the belief in an authority outside themselves, abdicating not only thinking but common sense as well. All of this knowledge is stored in your bloodline. In like manner your Bible claims that humankind was created by a Hebrew God around 4000 B.C., yet in ages long before then the true Gods, who are your ancient parent/creators, came here from all parts of existence. Their seed and their ideas have been transmitted throughout all of time, and traces of their existence can still be found in most places on your planet: North and South America, Australia, Indonesia, Asia, India, Europe, and Africa.

The landmasses have changed and moved over time. You believe these were gradual shifts and changes, yet today the theory of gradualism is losing favor because Earth is dancing with changes on geophysical and energetic levels. No one quite knows what to make of the changes because in most cases you choose to believe the official line of "truth." Your perceptual experiences indicate gradual change as the rule, and you cannot even imagine the knowledge that your ancestors accessed. They knew that sudden, shocking, and surprising changes can occur in an instant, and in that regard, you cannot make contingency plans.

Although your distant ancestors understood the use of their brains to a greater degree than you do, that is not to say they had full-brain capacity. They simply utilized the right and left brain in a more balanced way, as a survival tool. Over the last few thousand years, you have been discouraged from using the right or intuitive side of the brain. You have slowly become linear and left-brain oriented. Western civilization, where this bias is more widespread, is now branching out as a great empire around your globe, spreading its left-brain orientation that is disconnected from common sense and from a meaningful relationship with existence. Riddled with family secrets and secret societies, Western civilization is filled with lies, deceits, and manipulations that are only possible because you have lost the balancing influence of your greater selves.

Because of this imbalance your methods for dating time, including the carbon dating system, are errant. You do not take other factors into account such as: Many energies have the ability to shift and move through time. Time is not static; it is an ever-flowing river—ongoing and changing yet holding its own integrity. Can you understand the integrity of a drop of rain in the river? It mixes and blends, yet it is always itself—or is it? If it is part of the whole, can that drop be accessed in any part of the river? We want to stretch your imagination so that you understand the hologram where the whole can be stored in a part. Imagine a creature, a being so intelligent, alive, and intense that it is everywhere at once. Its essence is pure and responds to every other aspect of itself. This is a creature that vibrates curiosity and malleability, unique characteristics that allow it to be molded and to mold as well. And you must learn to dance with this energy.

One of the prophets on the silver screen of your world, Yoda, calls this creature the Force. It is a being alive and intelligent. Although this Force is benevolent, kind, nurturing, and loving—the most tender being you can imagine—it can also be dynamic and ferocious—dark, compelling, and even evil. It has all these sides. Sometimes you imagine an existence made of all goodness, a golden age where everything is perfect. Do not rule out the wounds of darkness that may take a while to heal. And do not rule out the opportunities to transform for those who are here to be transformed.

Many of you would like to take evil and step on it, destroying it like you would a bug. Squish, smash! Begone into another reality! This practice of eliminating human life because it is perceived as evil does you no good. In the end your history and experience are filled with war of one kind or another: humans fighting one another for the right to speak their truth and share their perception. And one human or another is always wanting to suppress someone else's ideas, someone else's thinking. This activity has been a foundation principle at the core of your being.

Today you must learn to respect the spiritual integrity of others—a raindrop acknowledging the river—by claiming your own inner authority and developing your character from it. As you learn to explore your psychic self, you will understand that "connectivity" comes with telepathy and that the Gods have always used telepathic communication with humans. Remember, during the Arian Age, the Gods were portrayed in the form of huge statues and monuments, all great structures of stone. The builders understood the importance of spirit and knew how to use sound to build these great structures depicting the Gods.

In the Age of Pisces, God became invisible and was pronounced no longer telepathically connected to you. If you claimed otherwise, you were burned at the stake or locked away in dungeons. Telepathy appears to be a "dangerous" potential lurking in your genes; yet your distant ancestors used it to see into another point of time, to travel out-of-body, and to view the Now, the Past, the Future simultaneously—to travel on the river of time. They understood sound and the power of their minds and conversed with the Gods. However, the Gods tricked them, as the Gods often do, and the humans gave their power away and worshiped the Gods rather than finding a place of equality among them.

And what is our place of equality with the Gods? you may ask. How will we ever be equal with the Gods? Must we develop our telepathic and clairvoyant skills, and our teleki-netic skills? It is easier than that: Your task is to vibrate with love to the best of your ability. Love your friends and love yourself, be nurturing and harmonious, and be at peace. This in itself is a great feat, one most of your ancestors never quite seemed to achieve. However, some of them did pass the test, creating what you would call Utopia. Where does Utopia dwell? Could Utopia dwell in the time line of Earth that you know? Is it possible to build a Utopia? Or would it simply arise of its own nature because of a natural tendency to rise to a higher frequency?

Everything changes when you start to emit your own frequency rather than absorbing the frequencies around you, when you start imprinting your intent on the universe rather than receiving an imprint or blueprint from existence. You are in a twenty-five-year window where humankind is at a testing ground, choosing a probable road in the great Book of Earth. Your ancestors had similar tasks, and now at this point you too have many roads from which to choose. We ask you to develop yourself along the lines of a whole being, with both male and female energies in balance with the right and left sides of your brain. Using the full vitality of who you are, imagine that everything your ancestors have been is stored within you, for it is with this knowledge that you must proceed forward.

Your ancient ancestors prior to this Piscean cycle tracked the movements of the planets and appreciated the opportunities the heavens heralded. They knew that intelligent beings visited periodically, and often that these beings were far superior to the local humans at the time. You are watched; you are maintained. We have suggested that twenty-six thousand years may be equivalent to one year to some beings. This does not mean that they are greater than you; it means they view reality from another perspective. These beings are, in your terms, multidimensional and know how to exist in a number of flows or calendars of time. Most of you mark time by the Gregorian calendar, which was created less than four hundred years ago. At the time the pope and other authorities of the Western world made adjustments and located all of the holidays at equinox, solstice, and the cross-quarter days. Slowly the markers of cyclical time were replaced with the Christian icons who now intercede for you with the Gods.

Even though the older meaning of cyclical time vanished, knowledge of it is still held deep within your cells; it is there. You must, however, stretch further back in time to find an even deeper meaning. Why did your ancestors mark time in this way? What was inside them that helped balance the Earth? Could it be the balance between the logical mind and the intuitive self that you so need to develop as you enter the twenty-first century? Your ancestors lived further back than the calendar you count and the few ages we speak of. They knew that sudden change would happen at the beginning or the end of an age, and that the ages marched backward in the zodiac to create the great cycles of time. Throughout the Great Year, the 26,000-year precession of the equinoxes, cycles keep moving and changing, and existence keeps expanding, everywhere available and present.

The Gods, in their need to experiment with and observe you, separated you. This is why you have various races on your planet. You come from genetic families, seeded by coalitions, agreements, and committees of various stellar beings; therefore you are considered to be biological storehouses by some. Many view you as laboratory mice: to be studied, shifted, and changed. This does not elicit a very pleasant feeling, does it? There are also those who view you with the kindest of intentions and who watch you flourish and accept you for who you are. Some see you as children who need parenting, and they are here to support you, not to punish you. They want to help you learn your lessons with kindness, as loving parents ideally would. They are like parents who find it important to spend time with their children, to communicate directly with them as the ancients did, rather than to park them in front of electronic tele-teachers as modern parents do.

In this twenty-five-year period, people from cultures all over the globe, from all genetic strains, will begin to realize that you now live within a window of opportunity, a fleeting moment. For you this period elongates seconds to minutes to hours to days; it is one of the unique features of this time. Linear thinking and linear experience trap you, as a rule of time, whereas multidimensional perception allows you to be in many lines and flows of time. Time can flow fast, slow, or not at all. Those you call Gods and Goddesses are multidimensional, as were some of your ancestors. However, in the management of minds, fear was chosen and multidimensional living was abdicated.

At the end of one age and the beginning of another, many dilemmas arise and the tools for living, for continuing civilization and continuing yourselves, are questioned. Today you are challenged to reestablish a high culture where life is once again valued, where mothers and fathers are honored because it is through their joining that all of you are born. When you begin to value your biological being, you will understand that there is such a fine spirit within you more valuable than anything you will ever create, a spirit that is priceless, a flame of light like a jewel—an emerald, or a diamond—with so many glittering facets that it seems to grow as you observe it. This is who you are. Priceless. Yet you keep forgetting your value or else you refuse to believe it and say, "This is not in the books of history; therefore you must be kidding us." You even think we must be buttering you up, sweet-talking you. Humans, priceless? Yes! You!

Reality mirrors itself. The Creator we ask you to contemplate is in all things. It diversifies and allows itself to be everything, everything that ever was and everything that will ever be. This vastness is really a unified field of love, and when you really comprehend this fact, you will relax into living. When you build the foundation of your development with these principles and live them each day, you will truly be inheriting and claiming your pricelessness. However, do not expect everything to be done for you. One of the most generous aspects of the creative force is to allow you to develop in any way you choose, to feel isolated or to feel connected, whichever you want. The creative force is you: an intelligent, biological, ever-present being seeking out the places you want and the times that excite you.

In ages long past, civilizations sometimes existed for a hundred thousand years, and there were others that lasted much longer. Utopian civilizations are etched in the annals of your memory and in ancient mysterious records that are kept by secret societies. Your ancestors continued to quietly write down these histories; they hid the ancient knowledge in art, music, and carved in stone. Utopias, as you consider them, would be places where humans and multidimensional beings came to interact and work out a plan where a certain harmonic frequency would be established. More often on your world you destroy one another. You merge and blend through wars of conquest, where you punish those at the bottom of the ladder or destroy one batch of humans to make another batch feel important. There has always been a possibility to blend peacefully, but you rarely choose it. Some choose it, of course, otherwise you would annihilate one another; yet your history is full of dead civilizations.

The Utopias though are more than alive. Although anything can be located on the stream of time, the Utopias do not come to an end. They could eventually stop, although sometimes the collective energies of the Utopias learn to manage their frequencies so well that they keep integrating more and more energies; and as they continue to vibrate, they appear from your point of view to literally disappear. They raise their frequency of compatibility and compassion, forms of tolerance, to a place where they see the perfection of light and dark. They would certainly not be all light in your terms; however they have integrated the so-called dark side and continuously work to transmute it. They allow a doorway of healing for the dark energies to enter into their world, and the dark energies come to be transmuted. Is this not an interesting concept?

This example could be considered a form of Utopia, a place that continuously exists in a state of nonjudgment. Now you may say to yourself, "Goodness, if this utopian place is filled with light and they allow a portal for dark to jump in, will they turn everything to light?" This is an important point to ponder. How much darkness is there to transmute? How much so-called evil is there in existence? And does darkness ever need to be transmuted? If darkness swirls itself into light, what does light swirl itself into? Perhaps these utopian cultures recycle light and dark into each other and have found a balance. Today you are also faced with finding a balance. As you explore the depth of spirit, some of you only want to find the good stories, the tales of light.

A great healing victory needs to take place on Earth. You have the potential to achieve and transmit the frequency of love, which will change everything, unify existence, and serve as a mirror of the great Creator. This is your potential now. If you would each send out a thought wave of intelligent creation from the vortex of Earth into all of existence, it would make a difference. Let everyone and everything know that love is possible and that you are truly alive and proud of it. When you are unified as humankind, the doors will open so that you can meet the rest of your family as equals, with your total psychic connection switched on so no possibility of deceit, chicanery, or deception can occur. We ask you to grasp this possibility, to go into your spirit and seed the core of your being with a new probability among the many threads of choice. Choose the one where you decide to be priceless, where knowing many things you live in complete comfort and relaxation. With the vibration of love, the purpose of the plan and its connections become more apparent. And then you can know that the darkness really inspires the light. It outlines it, giving it form and definition.

To be more at ease with who you are, picture the numeral 8 resting on its side and lying over your eyes, with a balanced flow of energy moving from one side to the other. When you want to know something, picture this figure over your eyes and send the energy round and round; then see yourself at the cross points, ask a question, focus, and see what comes to you. This is a technique from the Book of Earth that your ancestors used. They would balance both sides of the brain, then focus their attention in the area you call the third eye. Use the power of your spark of life to imagine and create, and remember your ancestors do indeed speak through your blood. This and other hidden mysteries have been used as the foundation of many secret societies, for without psychic abilities secrets can be kept.

In order to stop the secrecy and deceit on Earth, each of you must be willing to claim your great inheritance, your ability to feel. Have compassion for the ancestors of the last few thousand years whose fear-imprinting you now carry as a great armor. Remember that the test of all ages is always about the choice between producing the frequency of fear and the frequency of love. Perhaps you will become one of the utopian worlds, a place in the mind where only a specific frequency can enter. No time-jumpers, no matter how powerful or how accurate their set of coordinates, can ever enter a utopian time line. The lines are, in your terms, sacrosanct, secret, with only the proper vibration allowing entry. This is an important concept for you to understand because for a time you can create this vibration, this frequency on Earth. You must learn to find what you have in common with one another and then to unify. You will learn that what appears to tyrannize you, from inside or outside, is really there to test you. What frequency will you produce? Who will you be? Once you learn to produce a frequency of love, and learn to maintain and continue to be self-sustained by it, will you share it with others? Or will you write of its secrets in your books, as some of your ancestors did, and keep it hidden away?

Within the various continental structures around your globe, there lie many old artifacts, many clues and opportunities to understand the fuller picture of your origins. Artifacts have been uncovered over time, and many of them do not fit within your sequential view of the past. As we have said, you have developed linear thinking and shut off the knowledge of cyclical living, which not only punctuates the heavens with meaning but also serves to better describe time as flowing like a river, moving and moving and moving. Some artifacts appear to be mistakes, anachronisms found where they have no business being and yet, there they are. These out-of-time objects range from footprints of humans preserved in stone next to dinosaur prints, to gigantic human footprints and skeletal forms twenty feet tall or more, to vases and cups, batteries, jewelry, and spherical balls—to name a few. All kinds of devices have been found buried in the earth as people mined for minerals, excavated ruins, or just built roads. Sometimes these objects were found because someone was hunting for antiquities, and at other times they appeared as if by magic. Some were even found embedded in layers of stone millions of years old. These discoveries, of course, are not announced in your newspapers. The idea of sophisticated objects, like those manufactured today, being found buried in layers of earth millions of years old does not compute with you.

You are blinded by your beliefs, which shuts you down. You are in a state of denial, and as humankind you have been programmed to exist in this mind-controlled state. The more you believe in only a linear world, anything and everything existing outside your time line will be blanked out. You dismiss them, filing them away in the never-never land of unfounded notions, and think, "This is not what I was taught or what I was told." Now these objects are studied, of course, and sometimes turned over to museums or to collectors of out-of-time objects. Where do you feel the objects come from? Actually, Earth is billions of years old, and civilizations have been here from the beginning, seeded and guided by various celestial beings who experience time from a different perspective. And then there are time-jumpers who can move from one section of time to another.

These time-jumpers go into time to change history, but as we have said, not every slice of time is available to them. You are travelers on your planet, yet you cannot go everywhere. Every time you travel somewhere new, you must have the proper currency and learn the language and customs. There are many factors involved when you travel around your planet. Yet for time-jumpers, there are even more considerations. They have a multidimensional view of your world and of all of existence. They are not linear like you; linear beings often have their circuits blown when they experience a time-jumping. On your planet, people have walked down the street and slipped into another piece of time, sometimes onto the opposite side of the globe from where they were. People can shift dimensions easily, though it is not common; however the experience is certainly more common than you recognize.

Many people have these experiences and do not speak of them because they are frightened. In earlier times when there was less freedom of expression, if someone spoke of such a thing, they were locked up and called crazy. The shift from linear to multidimensional living is stretching each of you, so allow yourself to shift gears if it occurs, and say, "Oh yes, I can be me, never losing the integrity of myself while I simultaneously view and participate in another reality." This can be done with your biological being.

Time-jumpers come in all shapes and sizes with varieties from every aspect of existence. Certainly on Earth there are time-jumpers in the time in which you live—late-twentieth- and early-twenty-first-century Earth. People have been altering time on your planet for ages, although your current time experiments are the outgrowth of activities that began, as we mentioned, about one hundred years ago. There have always been those who could use their minds to tinker with electromagnetic energies and affect time. Where would they get these ideas? you may ask. Remember, the invisibles are all around you; multidimensional beings are in your world. You think the Gods have gone away; remember we said they are simply taking a nap or are actually playing a game of peekaboo with you.

Over time people became terrified of their inner abilities, and no longer had a natural telepathic link with the Gods. You must bridge this gap while simultaneously learning to bridge the gap in your mind from the right to the left side of the brain. A sense of whole being and living will result, allowing you once again to communicate with your Creators, your cohorts, family, and friends; simultaneously you will deal with the electromagnetic signals, the energies of an invisible sort used to confuse and stop the great awakening of your abilities and the claiming of your pricelessness. It is true. A great battle exists, a fight for the souls, spirits, and bodies of humankind, for the core of your being is so vital that many seek it. Keeping you in ignorance, most particularly in linear thinking, forces you to produce the frequency of fear rather than the frequency of your own natural biological inheritance, unique to you, which is the vitality of love. Love is not stored anywhere quite like it is stored in you because you are part of a library and are a priceless experiment as well.

You came from beings who seem to expand worlds, who create universes, beings so clever that all time exists for them at once. They charter time and leave clues as tidbits of knowledge stored away just in case they might need them. This is not so different than your custom of storing away money for a rainy day. Like squirrels storing their nuts for winter, the Gods stored their stuff, they stashed it away, hid it so they could have it when they needed it. They are not so different from you, you know. In actuality, as we look at the Book of Earth, you are all related and so they are to you. Yet in order to really understand these tales, you must feel separated for a while because of what you created: the whole separation of us and them. Ideally, by the end of our tales, you will have combined everything, coalesced it all with a great deep breath, a sigh of relaxation, knowing that the pieces of the puzzle of your life fit. Hidden meanings will then become apparent and the disconnectedness you formerly felt will be gone. As your living weaves into significance, the level of stress you live within is reduced.

As Family of Light, you are required to know and understand a panoramic view of existence that at this time too few humans can grasp and maintain. The Book of Earth will come alive in your eyes, in your memories, and in your bellies. Your belly is thought to be your body's second brain; actually it is the body's primary brain. Begin to trust your belly. Imagine that the intuitive part of yourself feels from there. You must learn to use all of the brain in your cranial area as well as the brain in your belly, the feeling place where you identify and relate to the outside world. This is the key to producing the frequency of love. If you do not permit yourself to be honest with yourself and to deal honestly with the simple things in life, then how can you produce love? Instead you will produce resentment because you will not mean what you say. Do you understand? By naming and dealing with the feelings that arise in this center, you can always move back to love by addressing what is really occurring. Your ancestors faced this challenge many times as they dealt with the Gods who came here and wanted to be a force of change for humans. Always, as we have said, fear, war, anger, victimhood, bloody death and killing, rape and pillaging, power over others, seemed to be the paths chosen.

You stand at the gates of that test once again. Remember the Roman Empire, bridging the Age of Aries to the Age of Pisces, and the Christed figure you revere as points in time— there were others before and after who brought opportunities, either for control or to set you free. You will never find your spirit, dear friends, inside of a structure. The structures you build to gather in to sing to the heavens or to perform your rituals of experience cannot contain the vastness inside of you. These tabernacles you call religious structures in actuality trap spirit. They serve as great generators where you give your spirit away and send energy to something else. Steeples and crosses act as antennas, you know.

Understand that the bridge you are building to the twenty-first century must be one where you raise your frequency. Call in the abilities of your ancestors; your bloodline is rich with wide varieties of who you are. You can also call on your ancestors as colleagues and friends. Many multidimensional beings come here now, some in friendship and others in deceit, because they are confused. Humans cannot be labeled and categorized into one behavioral type; some of you are quite aggressive and others are more than kind. Many of the beings come here to feel your vibration, to test you, and to become integrated by you. They do not mean for you to fear them. When you choose fear, you stop the flow of energy of those who work with you because your power ends where your fear begins. You must learn to manage your own fear and to manage your own moments by being in them. You will manage your own bodies by deciding that what you are is rightfully yours, and then you can change.

Within your spirit, the deepest part of yourself, a core identity exists that you must learn to access. The territory may appear to be a dark night of the soul where you will have to really examine this lifetime and the full retinue of your emotions. Perhaps other lifetimes will be included as well. As the lines of time open and you claim your psychic inheritance, relinquishing the fear of your ancestors, remember that you are part of a celestial family who both cherishes and ignores you, a family where some would do anything to extend your existence and others would destroy you in the blink of an eye. All of this the great Creator allows. Now imagine the bridge and see all of these beings drawn to it. Feel this happening inside the core of your being and imagine a flame of light inside yourself that never goes out. Use the act of breathing to activate the flame. See a powerful energy inside yourself that connects you with everything, with the vibration of love. The attention you place on your breath allows you to relax, to be in the Now, and to expand your field into many Nows.

It is very important for as many of you as possible to grasp the great task ahead. In the larger Book of Existence, this is just another task. However, in the Book of Earth it is a big task. In this day of your life and in this moment that you all live, it is a gigantic task, and yet you are not alone. Now breathe your vibration into your field. Breathe your common sense, your connection, your calmness, your love, into your lungs with your will, your power, and your intent. By the strength of your spirit, arising from the deepest core of your being, use the power of your mind to think for yourselves, to discern reality, and to call the word of your own command into being. *Speak, manifest, and live, dear friends, your true selves.*

The elasticity of reality is quite malleable. As Yoda said, "The Force both obeys and commands." Which will you do? Will you be commandeered by the force of electromagnetic change that sweeps late-twentieth-century Earth and affects all of existence? Or will you take your power and stand facing the storm, creating what you desire as you breathe in the power of the wind and feel it blow across your skin and through your hair? With the power of your will and your strength, with your intent and your desire, you can use the power of the changing times, the storms of Earth and the coming cosmic storms, as energy, as fuel to change your world.

The storms may appear to be here to destroy you. In actuality they unplug a system of control based on electronic and interdimensional tyranny, a dark occultism, a wizardry gone bad. The darker energy chases you and would do anything to divert this great power that rises in you, yet it is in dealing with the darkness that you find your power. Otherwise, dear friends, we see in the Book of Earth that many have been lazy, many have chosen fear or simply turned their backs on a great opportunity. And so the shadow that chases you actually defines your light.

As you develop into your being, at the core of yourself, be willing to face what is there. Do not judge it; rather unify and become one, understanding that your shadow, as it unfolds on your planet, is there for a purpose: to heal and integrate you and to take you into the greater responsibility of creating a Utopia, perhaps. Yes, perhaps out of late-twentieth-century Earth will spring forth one of those rarest of gems in the celestial records: a Utopia, a civilization so highly evolved that all life is valued, where everything everyone does is completely valued and honored. Here the balance of existence, the yin and the yang, the light and the dark, the black and the white, the day and the night, is seen in divine protection, divine perfection. And so it is.

The Peaks of Destiny

We remind you, the inhabitants of late-twentieth- and early-twenty-first-century Earth, that our purpose on this journey involves your destiny. We have spoken to you about the Book of Earth and how it can be accessed, where we Pleiadians and many others can look at you on the flow of time. You are alive in each moment of the past, the present, and the future, and can make a choice in each one of these moments. You are beginning to realize that Earth is consciously alive, aware, and connected to other great patterns and that there are ways of figuring out these patterns. This idea, when you come to understand it, will lead you to self-empowerment and self-discovery, perhaps even to the peaks of your own destiny. Our destiny, of course, is ours, although there are collective destinies, imprints from the heavens or what may be called the Grand Avenues of Time, and it is the collective destiny that inspires us.

The ancients on your planet, from cultures all over the globe, understood that there was an imprint, a map, in the heavens and that much of this belt or zodiac depicts animals. Remember, we and others see Earth as a place where knowledge has been stored in all creatures, in everything. Animals hold and represent another form of knowledge, a way of transcending linear time. Animals do not count time the same way you do; therefore they experience the world in a different way. The ancients understood more of Earth's true purpose. They knew that there is order in all things, even in chaos, and that how humans handle chaos is a test of their ability to evolve and change.

We ask you at this point to reflect upon yourself for a few moments. Ever since you have encountered our words and invited us into your life on this journey of change, what has happened? Reflect on the reality you have created and understand it as part of the process of change. Our words may seem innocent. We convey tales of the past, of cosmic knowledge, hidden secrets, and mysteries; we offer words of encouragement and empowerment as well as those addressing darkness, evil, and fear. Perhaps some of these ideas have created chaos within you. Perhaps your being, your thinking, and your life are changing. If so, then sit up straight, take a deep breath, and say to yourself, "Ah ha! The journey is on. I am on the path to change!"

The key for all of you to understand is that the path of change is unpredictable. When you invite new energies into your life and expand the way you view the world beyond a linear, prescribed manner, you begin to reach out sideways, backward, and forward, creating a different energetic pattern within your auric field. And you all have magnificent fields if only you would switch them on. As we said, your will, intent, and breath allow you to build the energy field through your bodies, expanding it into the ethers around you. Remember, the ether was understood by your ancestors; their marking of time and knowledge of the zodiac and the heavens allowed them to function in a practical way. Perhaps they did not have all of your conveniences; however we ask, "What do these conveniences really do for you?"

We want to assist you to place a greater focus on yourself, to claim your spirit, that flame of energy inside yourself, because this step is essential for your development. It is no easy task to perform, yet the formula is the simplest of all possible recipes. Simply combine your attention, your breath, your will, all aligned with your heart and your mind—the mind in your brain and the mind in your belly. Actually, by utilizing the wholeness of your being, you expand and fill your auric field, the bubble of electromagnetic energy around you, with who you are. This may be frightening at times, because the process of unfolding to personal understanding and development sometimes seems littered with more junk in the cellar, the closet, and the old barn out back than you ever realized. You do not completely grasp that you store so much inside yourself—so many feelings, so many responses to everything that has transpired in your life. You are a biological mechanism designed with impeccability and are being upgraded at warp speed by the great electromagnetic and cosmic waves that Earth is now passing through in space. These waves imprint you with knowledge from the zodiac belt, the library that houses the ancestral records in this realm of existence.

All systems have their belts of knowledge, which serve as another way of storing living data, and you fill your belt of knowledge constantly, with every thought you think. When you breathe with relaxation during the unfolding changes, you can connect with a vibration that accommodates rapid accelerated change. We give out this vibration and seek those who are willing to transmute themselves and rise to the great task of becoming energized vibrating beings in a world filled with poisons, toxins, and fears. These poisons come home with you in the grocery bag, and are sold on every street corner. Will you recognize them and create your own frequency? This is part of the great task that lies ahead.

We ask you to dive deeper into yourself and see who you are. Where are you going to take yourself? What are you going to do with your new vista and view of the world? The change that is upon you, like a fan unfolding, is just the beginning. Soon the fan will begin to move faster and faster, and ideally you will learn to know who you are and to find yourself during the process of psychic acceleration, where you become more astute and aware. The more you are willing to go inside and address who you are, to unite with the flame in the core of your being and to keep it burning with the faith that you are on a path of purpose, the more you will become a pioneer altering a paradigm that has been locked and frozen for thousands of years. Perhaps you are a ray of light, and from the quiet of your own home you melt the polar ice caps, and in the perseverance of your own being, you change the world. We ask you to be steadfast in the quiet of each moment, because your power lies in your every breath feeding the idea, the belief that you are a magnificent biological structure. You are timed, coded, designed, and planned to be activated to the height of your abilities in the Now. This Now, of course, is but a moment in time, a fleeting moment from our point of view. We have spoken of it as the junction point between 1987 and 2012, the bridge to the twenty-first century.

We mentioned early on that these tales were about the truth. We have learned that it is important to tell the truth from the beginning, from the middle, and from the end. This is essential for you to understand and is one of the tests you now face. What is the galactic truth: Who is out there, who are they, where did they come from, why are they here, and what do they want? Who is telling the truth? Why do all these stories conflict? Why are there so many Gods? Which God is God and whose God is God? Seeking answers to galactic truths will launch an era of new thinking, and this is the territory you must map.

You are pioneering this new territory, yet it is really no different than the territories your ancestors pioneered. They hacked their way across continents and built roads, houses, farms, and cities. In the process of exploration they discovered special energy vortexes, just as you are being led to natural bay or watershed areas of consciousness. If you imagine your globe in its ripe fullness, you will see there are natural waterways and harbors around most large cities. These areas are always entry points onto the land where there is safe harbor for ships, where ideas and commerce begin to grow. This form of development is how you, as a culture, experience yourselves; it brings the promise of growth and is how you learn. We offer you a metaphor for what your ancestors were dealing with so you can understand what you, as humankind, are to explore in the vastness of a so-called invisible, uncharted world. What harbors are you drawn to? What roads will you build and where will you pioneer? Where will you place your homesteads? And will some say, "Hey, don't live there, that's dangerous territory!" Where will the safe zones be? Will you cluster again in groups like your ancestors did or will you moderns map the territory in a new way, creating a new grid pattern through which humankind can interact?

In this moment take a deep breath, breathe into the very bottom of your lungs, hold for a moment, then exhale, completely emptying your lungs. Imagine your breath spreading out like a mist of energy filled with your intent. You can use energy any way you want. Remember, how you begin the journey and what intent you have will open the path of discovery that you will tread upon. So, once again imagine in your mind's eye the numeral 8 or infinity sign placed in the center between your brows. Activate that image as a part of yourself. When we speak to you of the test of the ages and cycles of time, imagine a pulsating mandala of energy, a kaleidoscope of shape and color taking form there. Feel it. It can appear to be another eye, an eye looking back at you, black in the center like your pupils, contracting in and dilating out. The iris is full of maps of your inner being. Use this inner eye to connect to your inner self, and as we address your development toward the peaks of destiny, which is where you can go with it, apply what we are sharing with you to facilitate the task of living in these accelerated, changing times.

From our point of view, there is only one place you can go in this moment and that is inside yourself. The changes that our words and energy bring forward allow you to know more about yourself and your patterns of behavior. The ways in which you map reality have become comfortable, keeping you where you are, and also allowing you to feel stuck or struggling. As you open to our energy, these patterns will begin to shatter. "Why, Pleiadians," you may ask, "do they need to shatter?" Well, we will say this with the kindest intent: You are stubborn to change. Your lessons keep occurring, and they speak to you loud and clear. And yet, blessed be, you cherished humans still have difficulty breaking out of ancient, ingrained patterns of sameness and mediocrity because you think "this is how I always did it." You do not seem to realize that everything you do creates reactions and has consequences because everything is connected.

One of the greatest abilities that we have acquired as time-jumpers, able to access the Book of Earth and the Book of Existence, is to translate to you the energy that opens the Library on Earth. As a result, you can be imprinted with this energy, then begin to access everything for yourself. How you get to the place of knowledge is to know yourself; what you do with your knowledge is yet to be seen. Feelings are your guide. Trust your feelings and learn to express them, and do not blame anyone for how you feel. Be yourself, observe yourself. Look to understand any crisis you have been in or will be in.

Crisis creates an opportunity designed to shatter patterns of rigid behavior, which do not fall away simply because you get up on a quiet morning and say, "Ah, today I will give up everything." That is a logical decision; the change we speak of occurs through your feelings, often through creating a crisis where you must use your will, heart, and mind to redesign your life. Crisis shatters your impenetrable field, which is like the casing around a young seed, and you must learn to trust that, when the casing opens, you will have a sprout to shoot up. Not all seeds sprout, you know. And in all fairness, not all humans grow to the fullest of their capabilities; however they all do sprout. All humans, no matter who or where they are, or what they are experiencing in every moment throughout all of the eons of time, add to the information in your great zodiac belt of knowledge that houses what happens in this realm of existence.

You do not have to rush out to buy books to study these subjects. Use your imagination. Go inside yourself to find out how you feel about what you are currently creating. If you have had an emotional experience recently that has opened you up to deeper feelings, congratulate yourself; do not judge your emotions. However we will remind you that feelings of victimhood, anger, and blame must be very carefully watched. It is fine to feel anger; however do not blame another for how you feel. When you hold onto feelings of anger, you never accept responsibility for your part in the drama, which then creates an invisible storm that sits on the coast of your energetic field affecting your physical body. The resentment and all of the emotions you stuff—related to your family, lovers, friends, employers, or employees—act as volcanos, hurricanes, tornadoes, tidal waves, and typhoons, blowing through your energy field because your unexpressed feelings feed these thoughtforms.

In order to know yourself, you must ask, "How do I feel about this?" "Why have I created this?" You must give up numbness to become very aware. There are patterns of destiny, and you are going to reach the peak of human destiny when you truly begin to vibrate with sovereignty and self-knowledge. Your technological world may assist that development; however it may also steer you away from it. You will access greatness by learning how to interact with others, seeing others as mirrors, and knowing that you attain the trueness of your own being through the connection with your family and friends. Technology in many ways isolates and compartmentalizes you; in the last five hundred years of the Piscean Age, it has certainly separated you from everything. You have become meaningless marvels and mindless wonders.

This separation is the shell casing from which you are emerging. Some of those shells come from childhood and some are also related to other lines of time. As you get to know yourself, use the tools of your breath, will, and intent and say, "I want to know who I am, to have peace with who I am, to accept myself. I am willing to change, to look at myself and admit this is how I am. I am not going to judge myself." Each year in this twenty-five-year period has an acceleration that allows you to enter more completely into the human inheritance, a state of being that contains the ability to see through your bodies, to be clairvoyant and clairsentient, and to have natural telepathic connections with all life, including with the Gods. When everyone has achieved human potential, it will be a very different world. Who will need newspapers? Will you keep records of your newfound abilities or will you understand that everything is imprinted in the zodiac, the ethers, the maps of the heavens, and that living and breathing in each moment are the records you keep?

Eventually you will be moving from a receptive mode that is receiving ideas from the cosmos and being imprinted by them to broadcasting ideas out: Around the year 2012 is your peak broadcast period. What will you broadcast? Ideally, all of the work you do today will allow you in 2012 to feel free, unencumbered, and in the vibration of love and forgiveness. You will embrace forgiveness not because you are generous and kind, overlooking the transgressions of others, but because ultimately your forgiveness will truly be backed by wisdom, an understanding that when anger and blame are in your field, they are the vibrations you continue to receive. You must learn to end the wars in your world by ending them in your minds. That is the true bridge to the twenty-first century.

The peaks of destiny call, asking you to unfold into a being that is magnificent; therefore, you must trust that when the casing breaks, you will sprout. In the springtime of consciousness before beauty actually unfolds, just as during the early springtime of your year, the Earth can look bleak and ugly. Yet you trust the change of seasons no matter how tumultuous they are, because there appears to be an order in Nature connected to the rotation of the Earth in relationship to the movements of the sun and the moon. Rains, winds, and fires awaken what has been dormant. You take Nature for granted, yet if you look at the miracle of it, you would see yourself, for you are a human seed sprouting. Perhaps just before your casing shell breaks, you feel the tightness of a dark, confined place; you may feel as if the casing will suffocate and destroy you. Will you allow your seed sprout to die inside because the casing feels tough and hard? The truly intelligent seeds help create the weather. The seeds propagating Earth know themselves very well and send out frequencies to call in what they need as long as the people around them love the land. If people stop loving the land, the seeds and the plants have a harder time utilizing their own vitality during the great weather changes you are now experiencing.

As you get to know yourself, there is much to examine: what you eat, your focus of intent, how to deal with all of the new discoveries and the sudden changes that are occurring everywhere, not just in individual lives but on a mass scale. Remember that violence will be sold to you, so find those violent or angry places inside yourself and set them free. Think of situations and people that still cause an angry reaction—in this and other lifetimes—then acknowledge wherever you happen to find this feeling. Now take a deep deep breath and using your conscious intent fill your whole body with the vibration of peace and love. Set free those you still hold as prisoners of anger in your etheric field. Take another deep breath and breathe into your field; let those people know that they are no longer prisoners of your mind. As you release them feel the result of the clearing in your field. Those who remain offer an unseen lesson and are the ones you truly need to set free in order to purge vibrations of anxiety, fear, resentment, or blame from your being. Those beings, as energies, must realize their freedom as well, so tell them, "Yes, it is time to go, you are out of my field, fly free. I no longer hold you to blame, I realize there are lessons to be learned. And, as I set you free, send back to me what you are learning so I, too, can continue to grow." Do this release now and feel the resulting vibrational change move through your field.

Do not be afraid of purging or detoxing. Heaven knows that you are living in a toxic world; everything is toxic. Cockroaches have been living in and adjusting to a toxic world for millions of years, and they have survived. We have often made a joke and said you could model yourselves after them. The insect world is far more adaptable than you; they also communicate by creating a frequency and do not need to write down their words. Animals are psychically connected and can deliver messages, which is why they were revered by the ancients, who knew the animals held parts of the zodiac as their provinces. There have always been those who could access the great libraries of the mind, the libraries of the ethers, and you are now building a bridge from the core of your being out into the ethers, where you will get to know who you really are.

If detoxification or purging takes place in your life, allow yourself to go deep into your feelings to discover what you must give up. The sprout gives up its protective shell. What have you been using to protect yourself? Usually protection takes on a form of isolation that keeps you separate. Seeds know they are in the ground and look forward to the time when they must burst their way through the dark soil and attract the rays of the sun; they know they are called forth by the sounds of the insects that scurry across the earth. The insects remind the seeds below the surface, through sounds much like ancient drumming, that it is time to come forward. Seeds, like all things, respond to sound. Your world is full of sound, some of which you hear and some you do not. As moderns, you listen to artificial sound created from instruments you have constructed, yet you would get much more mileage out of listening to the sounds of Nature, aligning with the Earth and going deeper into the mysteries and teachings of her technology.

Some of you scoff at this advice; you think the bugs and snakes will bite, or that it is scary out in Nature and something dark and unknown will grab you, or you might even get abducted. Not enough of you truly appreciate the natural world; you want to visit state parks rather than making your own backyard a park, or your own communities distinguished places of beauty. Turn off your motors and air conditioners, put on your walking shoes and get outdoors and take a holiday in Nature. Pay attention to all of the creatures of Earth: insects, birds, and creepy crawlies that walk and tumble on four legs, for they create a vibration that can help you bridge the gap to intuitive living, which is the way they live. Once you have cleared your field of anger and blame, open to the intelligences in the ethers around you, and their vibrations will help shift you into a new awareness of living.

If you can grasp the idea that you live in a significant world, and that you affect it by how you feel and what you think, then you can begin to change your experience in a most miraculous way. Awareness begins as a desire, which grows like a seed that shoots up from the ground and follows an innate pattern. You each have a pattern inside you, inherited from your ancestors: their abilities, tendencies, hopes, wishes, and fears. You must get to know the inside of yourself. You may find that you do not need certain patterns anymore—junk in the cellar or attic, dark and nasty stuff. When you throw it out, do so with love—your junk may be someone else's treasure. In the housecleaning of who you are, you will discover that you have certain feelings or more abilities than were ever acknowledged. Many of you will find that you are already switched on, that you have had these intuitions all along, although no one helped you understand them. Perhaps you were afraid of what you saw, or were told to be quiet about it. Remember, many of these knowings are not necessarily solid, static, defined events.

This unfolding of change and getting to know yourself will accelerate your energy fields, which will begin to connect up with the fields of others. You put out your own radio waves, just like the sun. Actually, you are becoming like suns. The sun and the moon are telepathic modulators that affect your thinking. The cycles of light and dark are charted through time, and just as you turn on a lamp at night to light the darkness, so do the sun and the moon. These bodies affect you in that way—lights on, lights off—and the light and dark modulations send information and energy.

When you explore the invisible territories of consciousness, you will set up camp in certain areas of thinking because this energy will sustain your field. You will find as you explore everything about yourself—both light and dark—that this process will accelerate a great shift toward the exploration of light and dark on the planet. All cards will be put on the table; all secrets and hidden mysteries will be revealed in 2012. This is needed so the final decision, the final counsel of frequency, can be achieved. Remember, by the year 2012 your task will be to transmit whatever vibration you have become onto the horizon of existence.

At a galactic conference, there are those who wait for you to march on stage to see your presentation. Many lobby to create a certain delivery; therefore, much shuffling occurs

around this great presentation, similar to the political shuffling that occurs in all branches of business and in the World
Management Team. Imagine that activity happening vibra-
tionally. As we have said, there are beings—human and otherwise—who want to manage your vibration. Remember that
the abdication of your thinking and psychic abilities is how
your frequency has been managed. Over and over again that
is the test in the Book of Earth. Will this batch of humans, living on this unique teaching sphere, a resplendent storehouse
of knowledge, will they use the sphere of life to build the
bridge of knowledge from one age to another? Or will they
once again give away their power because of fear?

Your DNA is altering and changing as every breath you
take affects the cells of your being. You do not have to rush out
and have yourself enhanced, although a little body or energy
work will certainly speed up the process. Breathing in the moment and using your intention will activate your inner power.
Call in the Goddess, the source of life, the feminine energy, for
she is truly missing in the imbalance of your world. She can
help you live in balance as male and female beings, understanding that your ancestors spoke with the Gods and knew
that they took many forms, that they were multidimensional
shape-shifters, existing sometimes as humans, or animals
sometimes taking the form of snakes, serpents, dragons, and
reptiles. The ancient legends are full of the tales of dragons
and their ability to merge with the mineral kingdom and their
preference for crystalline structures. They flew in the heavens
and swam in the oceans and walked the Earth. They were
your real ancestors. However, if you read books about these
creatures, you might think that they were imaginary because
you do not see them in your world today. Remember, your ancestors did not live in an electronically separated, meaningless
world. They lived with Nature: A free biological technology of
spiritual energy was around them, energy that had its own
channels to surf, its own virtual realities. Your ancestors un-

derstood, and your animals remember. Now you too must learn to implement this knowledge.

It is time to come forward as a magnificent biological structure. As you read our words, think of your favorite flower and bird, and hear the bird calling the flowers and the plants to grow. The animals of the world and the sounds they make, the sounds of Nature, are calling you forth as well. When you replicate these sounds on tapes or in movies and videos, it is never quite the same because you cannot replicate Nature. It is essential that you explore the vibrations of Nature. Your technological advances divert you in actuality from the truest understanding of who you are. Technology cannot replicate Nature, just as it cannot replicate love. These two experiences—Nature and love—are gifts that you can only seek out by knowing yourself and trusting the world around you.

Using the love vibration in relationship to other living beings will teach you how important it is to love yourself. These are easy words to hear, but they are difficult words to truly grasp. Many of you are great givers of gifts. How good are you at receiving? If the idea of having others do for you, give love to you, take care of you, and help you out of the goodness of their hearts, is frightening, then perhaps you need to open up to this idea. It is fine to be self-sustaining, a prime supporter and provider for yourself; however do not shut out others in the process. You will only get to know who you are by surrounding yourself with other people. As we have said, reality mirrors itself, and without other people what will you use for your mirrors?

Remember, you choose when to be born, your own divine moment; you map yourself through eons of existence, and then by some fixation of reality, you forget. You forget so you can live. Periods of living with forgetfulness have their tests within corrals of being, and now the corrals are being knocked down because the winds of change are here to disperse your thinking, your perceptions, and your ideas of yourself. You must learn to believe in your own uniqueness, your ability to create, for genius is sprouting inside of you. It is important to love yourself and love what has happened in your life, to vibrate with a frequency of acceptance and understanding and to find the lessons within experience. This attitude will create wellness in your being; for loving yourself enhances your immune system, changes your cells, and allows you to become immune to toxicities, because the frequency of love is the most powerful force in existence.

When sharing ideas with you, we use the opportunity to trigger your consciousness into deeper exploration. As you read our words, understand that within them are hidden meanings and codes—like the hidden meanings and codes in the rays of the sun. Language holds a multitude of avenues of expression and understanding. There are codes everywhere, and as you expand your consciousness and discover the uniqueness of each individual in their own experience of creating the world, you will see language and personal expression in a whole different light. Get to know yourself, believe in yourself and claim a code of integrity based on responsibility, accountability, and reliability. Remember, responsibility is your ability to respond to living. Deal with what you create because honesty will be required by all.

In the midst of understanding yourself build your foundation on love; it is your calling card, your identity card. As you explore the corridors of time, the stream of existence that calls you to understand more of who you are and to awaken to a greater membership in living, many lessons are at hand, so we suggest that you follow the impulses of day-to-day living that fit in with your standards. Use your will and intent to call for the mysteries of Earth's stories to be revealed through all peoples and their legends. Then you must learn to trust your whole body and ask, "Does this fit?" "Is this a spin on what to think and believe?" Remember, the truth is important, and the truth is always based on your experience and perspective.

As you open to who you are, you will open to many possibilities. Your blood is as rich as gold; it is the vitality of love that moves through your being, the blood of creation, of designed living biological beings. Everything will come alive, and understanding frequency will be the key. Learn to keep your own frequency as you explore the frequency of your ancestors. Ground yourself in the common sense of living and learn the day-to-day lessons. You can change into a beautiful, vibrant human being, so let that seed inside you sprout and send your roots down deep in existence. As a human being, know that you are here to live and that everything you meet in your day-to-day experience is part of the lessons in living. You can turn your lessons into toxic poisons or you can find the frequency of love inside yourself, turning all situations into a loving lesson of opportunity; it is all up to you.

In the Book of Earth, a probability exists where diamonds are found on the side of the stream. They have been dredged up from the earth and are there for the picking, if you have the courage to cross the brambles and the swampland and enter the dark underground tunnels you must journey through along the way. We ask you to consider taking the journey in which you find the diamonds, where opportunity is multifaceted and glitters, showing you your wealth as a creator. As you expand your field of perceptions, you will know why some of your ancestors, when they confronted the witches, the black sheep, and the renegades, forgot to use love and used destruction instead. Fear was present then and fear is with you again today, although this time you are not going to buy it. You are becoming wise, dear friends. Trust that.

So maintain your wits and your humor, and see yourself as a purposeful being. Love yourself and feel the fan unfolding. And if, when you go to sleep at night, you feel like looking into the Book of Earth, make the intention. Then, cloak

your body in a field of light based on love so you feel protected, grounded, and safe; next follow a spiral of light into
the ethers to see if you can read from the Book. It is a vast
Book with many lines of time that splinter and diverge into
separate directions. Long ago there were one or two trunk
lines, then they began to fragment over the ages, as every age
creates a change. Now as you approach another changing of
the ages, the lines are ready to move. The web will get very
crowded as more and more lines occur. Imagine weaving a
huge fabric that began with two or three strands of thread and
then began to grow and grow and grow. If all the lines stayed
separate, then the threads would not weave together and the
fabric would fall apart, because once there is that much fabric,
it must interweave and intertwine to make a new tapestry of
being.

We ask you to know yourselves; in so doing the energies
of creation will honor you, connecting you to the Family of
Living, to the Family of Light, to those who choose to believe
there is significance and purpose in all of existence. Embrace
these ideas and prepare yourselves to go much deeper into a
journey where you will become the true healers of your
planet, as you understand the power of love, the power of sur-
render, the power of compassion. You truly are connected,
and your frequencies will ignite each other and electrify the
night like fireflies on an early summer evening. We remind
you that there is a pattern, a purpose: Alone, you each hold
light; together the lights cluster and make patterns. Trust that
whatever you are dealing with, whatever doorway to crisis
you experience, it is leading you to a greater lesson in living
where ideally the power of love is what you learn. Forgive,
and broadcast your excitement to be alive.

Nothing Is Exactly as it Appears to Be

At this time in your personal development, as you build the bridge to the twenty-first century, a bridge that ideally will strengthen your inner knowledge and purpose, it is most essential for you to understand the territories to which you will be journeying, pioneering, and traveling. These territories are uncharted for you and do not have signposts, yet are not necessarily new territories because your ancestors and others have understood this terrain.

You consider your concepts about yourself and the world as factual and wish all of the world to conform to what you have been told or what you choose to believe. This is a noble way that allows you to conduct yourself in the world. However, seasons change and because you are on the cusp of great change for all of humankind, it is our intention to assist you to feel at ease with this change, which occurs on every level of existence and in every cell of your being.

How you view yourself in time and what you have been taught to believe will both be crucial elements in building the bridge in your mind to traverse experience, and to utilize this fleeting moment when humankind is being reorganized from its core to sprout into magnificence. If you can be nurtured to come out of your shells and if you crack the casing of rigid beliefs that surrounds you, as those beliefs fall away you will be transformed. This emergence is the healing work that all of you will perform over the next number of years: Getting to know yourself at such a deep level will allow you to feel at peace, to produce a vibration of being at ease.

Even though you know the effects of vibrations and frequencies, sometimes you forget and slip into bouts of depression or bad moods, or you project your anger onto someone, and then your patterns have to be shattered again. Seeing your fellow humans create one dire situation after another, have you wondered why people are creating so much toxicity in their lives? Well, consider that the challenges in living and the intensity of emotional interactions are greater than ever. The choices for fear also seem to be all around you, and this also is part of your self-realization process.

Your health and well-being must be your choice. The dips in life, the so-called down times, are designed to buff you, to take you into the carwash or tune-up shop of life so you will come out shining and running again. Many of you experience great fear when your bodies malfunction. Remember the prisoners of anger that you hold in your field? Well, it is most important to cleanse your field and to be grateful for who you are, for that is one of the tests you were born to master. Will you forget your lesson and be a grumbling victim holding a vibration that attracts more and more of its kind? Or will you trust the whispers of meaning, significance, and purpose that are awakening in all of you? What you do and think are connected to everything around you: the Earth, the animals, the weather. You paint the landscape you experience day in and day out, so begin to paint masterpieces of your lives, truly debunking limited thinking and fear as your only options in living.

How will you, as Family of Light, achieve the vibration

and create a new song of humankind's existence? There is only one way: You will do it by changing your own life and by claiming health to be yours. The releasing of anger is one way you can regain your health. You must pay attention to your physical vehicle and realize that it is changing, that all of humankind is changing. Your habits, the way you breathe, how you sit, the way you eat and sleep, all need to be reevaluated. It is time to change your schedule and let your body's callings be the guide.

As you claim yourself and build a bridge in this fleeting moment of opportunity, it is important to understand that evil cannot be eradicated. What you call evil has a purpose, and sometimes the same tools can be utilized to access either light or dark energies. We have referred to the dark side of living as Family of Dark. Over the years we have joked, saying no one writes, "Dear Pleiadians, thank you so much for mentioning us. I am a member of Family of Dark." Everyone claims membership and kinship to Family of Light.

We use names because you like names. You are coded for sound and words, and so our words make sense to you, and you say, "Oh, yes, yes, this sounds good. This fits my understanding of reality." Remember, words always mean more than what we say or what you hear or see. Words are really layers of symbols and can be used to convey hidden meanings. Your ancestors frequently used the symbols of stars, suns, moons, and serpents in their pictorial depictions. In the last one hundred years or so, archaeologists have uncovered ancient metal statues from the ruins of past civilizations where metalwork had not yet been developed. Many of these statues and statuettes depict strange beings wearing helmets adorned with circles and triangles, and with serpents on their helmets and in their hands.

Perhaps you believe that your language no longer contains such symbols. When you begin to understand frequencies, your vision will change, and you will see plans within plans and meanings within meanings. Significant living will unfold to a greater extent. Synchronicity describes a meaningful unfolding of events that are experienced without apparent order, a so-called divine intervention. When these experiences can be understood in terms of your connection to the ethers, how you create realities, and how your multidimensional selves and guides are all in accord, you will then be able to remap yourselves into a whole new vista of living.

It is important to understand the reason why you may be receiving messages through your body about your health. Your body is the easiest way for spirit to talk to you when you will not listen. Signs, symbols, and messages are all around you, and you must learn to interpret them. Your body is working with you, not against you, and right now, no matter what it is doing, your body is assisting you to learn something. Perhaps you are speeding up or slowing down. Do not judge. Allow yourself to feel lousy if you feel lousy, get in touch with it and really feel lousy. And then, when you start to feel better, energize the thought, "I feel better." Learn to express the feelings that come up from inside of you, and in this way you can be your own healer. Energy exists around you, and if you would let it in, it would cleanse and revitalize your body no matter how toxic the world may be. Applying this concept is a huge test to pass and a gigantic Grand Canyon of an idea to bridge. No matter how toxic the world is, will you detoxify it by creating the most valuable substance in existence: a love that you can generate for free if only you would get on with the task? We remind you of these concepts because you must be healthy journeyers, fully aware that your body is here to teach you lessons. You are not here for someone else to save you. You take lessons in driving cars and how to cook gourmet foods; however you do not really study the ways and means of affecting your physical body. Your ancestors had a greater understanding of the body than you currently do. For one thing, they knew that everything growing around them—

the green plants, vegetables, and fruits—affected them. They saw the plants as more than simply food to offset hunger or to fill an empty belly. Everything you grow has a vibration and by eating it you become one with that vibration. Some of the vibrations are compatible and others are not; however you select your food based on how good it tastes and not on its vibration. All plants and animals are vibratory beings, just as you are.

Your body is now going through a fortifying process that affects your cells because of the energies coming through the cosmos as electronic pulses, photons, solar flares, and magnetic and electronic waves. You are electromagnetic beings; your brains are filled with magnets. As electrical and magnetic fields shift, your body is deeply affected. Now, you can call 911 and say, "Help me, save me, fix me! Stick something in my body so I don't have to deal with this." Once in awhile emergency help may indeed be life-saving and life-altering; however calling 911 is not always the answer.

When you are in a health crisis, you can bring spirit into form by understanding that a test is occurring concerning your parameters, beliefs, and ideas about living. Let the old structure crash and crumble and imagine that you are like a set of Tinkertoys or Legos, which can be dismantled and rebuilt. You can do the rebuilding through love by accepting the changes happening in your life. When you are ill, you are often psychically very open because the field of energy around you is shattering, and your beliefs about the world no longer work. You often become ill by either putting storms in your field and not cleansing them, or by refusing to change. Your field then cannot withstand these great pulses of energy because you resist rather than allowing the energy to pass through your field and body, which creates change. When you stick with the same old routine, acting like a bull pounding its hooves, bellowing and refusing to move, then the resistant force grows stronger and stronger. Energy both follows your commands and controls you, depending on how you use it.

You are all healers, here to heal yourselves and to manifest the healing vibration so that plants, animals, and the Earth can feel the vibration running through the land. Many so-called witches in ancient times were simply those who understood the plants and, as midwives and herbalists, were sought out because they knew which plants would alleviate specific ailments. If you listen to the plants, you will learn that they symbolically represent various parts of the body. As you allow more energy to enter your body, and as you use the numeral 8—or sign of infinity—over your third eye, you will learn so much more and truly begin to relax and change with the unfolding times. Areas you formerly found boring will become fascinating because you now understand the information and will wonder how you could have missed it earlier. The cells of your body are timed to awaken, and now you are unfolding rapidly, blossoming to the fullness of your being. As you blossom, we ask you to heal yourselves, to allow the energy that is around you to sustain you as you forgive and let go.

Family of Light is here to set precedents and create options, to show alternate ways, not to declare one way as the only way. No dues, club memberships, certificates of approval, or graduation diplomas are required. You simply live, creating a vibration and a standard of living that astounds those around you. Many people who do not understand the times are afraid of the power running through humankind today, so they perceive some people with power as being arrogant. Be cautious of this fault and, as you unfold to the power of healing and the energy that is within you, be sincerely gracious. Do not snub or look down at those who have not yet discovered their abilities, because the energies are here for all people. All of you who have made the discovery are to inspire others to do the same.

At this time on Earth, you are part of a very special collective of humans. Each and every one of you, in every corner of the globe, came here to experience and to contribute to the vibration that would be broadcast during this fleeting moment of time. You are Family of Light and Family of Dark simultaneously existing here, supporting and allowing each other to play out your own dramas. Family of Light, do not worry about Family of Dark, for they will take care of themselves. The more you worry, the more likely you will end up at their reunion in 2012. Actually it would not be such a bad thing; you would find that they are similar to you. Do you think Family of Dark worries whether they will end up at your reunion? They cannot even conceive of it.

You are engaged in a frequency polarization, like a teeter-totter crazily going up and down, or a battle where you are each afraid of the other. The Light is afraid of understanding the Dark, the Dark is afraid of understanding the Light. What are Light and Dark, and what did the ancients think of their difference? We see that as you heal yourself and make peace with what is Light and what is Dark in your life, you will begin to understand what the ancients knew. The ancestors lived with the forces around them; sometimes for long periods of time, those forces would disappear and then return from the heavens, coming through the dimensions or through peoples' pineal glands, there again to interact. From every culture, there are stories and legends of these beings, flying in the skies in all sorts of vehicles. Imagination? Legend? Myth? Why do you believe certain depictions of your ancestors and scoff at others? For recognizable pictures, you say, "Ah yes, this is a bison. This is an antelope. Here are crops, and this is a fire." You pretend that the inexplicable ones are foolishness, an ancient pop art or science fiction on walls. Yet, as you look around your world, you see that yesterday's science fiction is becoming today's reality.

Many science fiction writers are in actuality great seers and visionaries who are able to perceive probable futures and lines of time where events exist. If this seems preposterous, remember that every thought you think creates a reality some-where; thoughts cluster together and exist with a frequency and aliveness, a velocity and vitality that you do not under-stand. Yet you will very soon, for understanding will continue to unfold in you, linking together symbols, signs, inner mean-ings, and codes that you will find at the core of all knowledge.

Mathematics, an abstract language, holds a key, and all modern-day science, whether traditional or quantum, is based on mathematical principles. What is behind the theory and numbers in math? Can theory really be proven or is it simply a pathway, a cluster of consciousness that appears to work in the abstract and occasionally is seen to fortify 3-D reality? Humankind will begin to expand its abstract thinking and the old abstract language of mathematics, upon which your sci-ence is based, will be seen as limited. Your modern-day scien-tists have turned the nature of existence into something extremely complex; once they understand the codes and sim-plicities in numbers, a new vista will open to them.

The universe is coded in the simplicity of your cells and in Nature. This will be made clearer by cloning. "Finally," your scientists are declaring, "we can clone sheep." This is really no big deal since humans have been cloned for a long time. Ancient manuscripts, including your Christian Bible, say that man was made in God's image. Perhaps this reference will mean something different to you once you understand cloning. Perhaps the original humans were cloned from be-ings you call Gods. Your science has much to discover about cloning because you do not factor in the life of spirit. It is pos-sible to replicate life; the question is, will spirit, the vital force, that flame of energy inside, inhabit a clone? Experimentation with cloning has occurred for millions of years. Remember, you are an ancient race.

We have asked you at various points to focus on different segments of time. In the Now, what is happening with your body, your attitude about it, and your initiation into being a healer? Being a healer allows you to reinterpret what you believe happened to you, and as a result your body shifts within the energy fields around you as you begin to clean out the old movies, videos, and fairy tales that you still build your life on. Allow their images to be released. And seeing beyond the Now, we want you to imagine a bridge to the twenty-first century, while you also hold in your mind the last five hundred years of history back to the Renaissance era. Feel the result of the great changes that transpired on your planet, and how over time people began to build and build in number to the late-twentieth-century's six billion humans. Remember, it is this particular period that introduced the educated to the idea of separation from the whole, resulting in insignificant living. Now, reach further back in your memory to about one thousand years ago and the time of the Middle Ages, and then further still to the time of the Dark Ages, which prevailed from about A.D. 500 to 1000. Five hundred years before that marks the beginning of the Piscean cycle with its seed of limited thinking, where compromise and political chicanery were the rule. The mysteries and teachings of significant living were overshadowed by a dispersement of energy from the Roman Empire, the Old World Order.

Holding these sections of time in your mind, realize that all of the preceeding ages of 2000- to 2200-year slices of time hold lessons as well. Can you imagine that your ancestors lived in slices of time that you are looking to heal, refurbish, reexperience, and energize? Approximately five hundred thousand years ago, energies visited your planet—and are returning today. Of course, these beings existed before that time and have been returning since then; however your lessons in living are always similar, no matter which piece of time you examine. The ancients, your living ancestors of Earth, filled their stories and myths with reports of battles in the heavens, of flying dragons and serpents, of balls of light, and with Gods who fought with sound or fire and lightning, with Gods who created energies that could not be understood. These beings, who came through the heavens, are part of the Book of Earth. Indigenous cultures hold sacred their celestial stories claiming kin to various star systems in the heavens. This ancient knowledge was passed down when the most important of abstract truths were etched on walls and tablets in symbolic form for you to decode today.

The snake is a prominent symbol used all over the world, adorning the thrones of popes, pharaohs, kings, and queens—royalty of every continent as well as tribal chiefs and shamans, both ancient and modern. It is also the symbol of your medical profession. The image of the serpent has been covertly woven into every aspect of your life without you understanding its true meaning. The image of the snake holding or biting its tail is a symbol for the Goddess and her creation of life: The snake is coiled in the shape of the circle or oval—the vulva, the entryway into the female organs of life. These symbols exist everywhere on your planet. Your ancients understood the powers of fertility and sexuality in relationship to the Gods, as well as what it meant to be in the body, knowing what the body did, that it could produce life or illness, experience both sensations of ecstasy and of great pain.

Religious structures, and actually many buildings, both ancient and modern, are adorned with the secret symbols of fertility. Oval windows in churches and great steeples on top are reminiscent of your own sexual organs. Why is it that these structures are often topped with a cross? Remember, the cross is an ancient symbol to mark a way, and in some traditions the crossroads depict where energies meet. Witches were said to gather at the crossroads because power was amplified and exchanged there. The cross is also an antenna; when it was used to crucify people, it broadcast pain into the ethers. In order to expand your perception, symbols and ideas need to be considered in a very neutral way, for some of you have far too many attachments to what you believe is the truth.

Truth is based on one's perspective and, ideally, as your perspective changes, you will discover new founding truths.

We purposely direct you to your body, toward creating a fountain of health and following the impulses that lead to healthy living—emotionally, physically, spiritually, and mentally—so you can fill the ethers with a vital vibration. The more of you who become healthy and broadcast that vibration, the easier it becomes for others to do the same. Remember, you are in a polarization here. Family of Dark would have you believe that poison, suffering, and pain are the only options, the only choices. When you choose these options, you are broadcasting that frequency into the ethers without consciously realizing it. The choice of peaceful, purposeful, and responsible living is always there, if you choose to focus on it.

It is important to understand that in healing your physical form, by making yourself grounded and whole and learning how to build a firm foundation of health, prosperity, and love in your vibratory field, you can then stretch out the branches of your blossoming self and grasp what is happening in the rest of existence. Without firm roots into the living life of Earth, you will be blown away in the winds of change. And yet the energies that would knock you over and shake you up are, in actuality, here to fortify you. You must find the grace to accept with dignity and gratitude the great lessons that you are creating. Learn from them. The solutions are always very simple and are usually right there in front of you, and they often involve doing the one thing that you resist doing the most. Your lessons often involve humbling yourself, saying you were wrong or asking for or giving forgiveness. These are some of the hardest tasks for humans to perform. Given ten thousand guns, you would gladly go out and fight a war. But forgive yourselves or someone else? A momentous task. The barriers seem greater than the Great Wall of China, insurmountable, going on forever. Nonetheless, you now are faced with meeting those walls or patterns of isolation that the Gods laid down for you.

When you begin to rebuild and fortify your field, especially if it has been shattered, it is essential to use this technique: Breathe a field of energy around yourself that is shaped like an egg or a sphere. If you want to use another geometric design, that is fine. Fill the shape with the intent of what you want to experience and of who you are. Learn to create using the vibration of love, for this is your true work. Your health and your work are one and the same. When you build the frequency of who you are, what you want, and what you want to experience in your auric field, it links you then with meaningful 3-D occupations. You must, however, first do the work in your field.

A truly fine healer understands that reality always delivers its messages and that lessons land first in the emotional field and then in the physical body. Initially you may have a mental idea and then emotionally experience it, yet it occurs in the field of your energy because it is a spiritual lesson. The energy around you that we refer to as Spirit, ether, or the energy of life, can either command or obey you. Sometimes this energy commands you to deal with situations, or possibly an opportunity is presented through adversity or loss. Cleverly disguised messages are hidden in every aspect of living. A healer can sense the messages in your field and suggest the necessary changes before the energy turns to ailments in the physical body. The discomforts and dis-ease that may move through your physical body are there because you did not deal with them in the mental or emotional body, or in the ethers. We ask you please to listen to the messages, the lessons spirit wants you to experience. Ideally, your empathy will grow through your own experience and this in itself is a great lesson in living.

As you understand your capabilities and what is being asked of you, do not burden yourself by wondering *how* it will all transpire. As we look through the Book of Earth, we see that the energies sent to you are yours for the receiving. Be open to the idea that you are living in the greatest time of change, and as you receive these energies, let them fortify you as the memories of your ancestors begin to run through your cells, calling through time for all to be healed. In this fleeting moment of existence, the power that runs through human-kind is remarkable, vast, impeccably rich, astounding, mag-nificent, magnanimous, and truly wholesome.

And as you awaken to who you are, many will want the same vibration. You must walk carefully; do not think it is your job to save everyone. There are low-energy people, vam-pires, who would steal your energy, draining you as if they were vacuum cleaners and leaving you wilted and withered. Be alert to this practice. Your job is to expand your frequency, to recirculate and recycle the energy that is all around you, to become a generator of free energy while using it as building blocks to design what you want, and to inspire others to do the same. The best healing you can give to others—whether through the lines of time with your ancestors and your Gods, or here and now with your family, friends, or neighbors—is to feel compassion for the lessons that they are all currently learning. To truly feel for another, you would say, "Oh, I've been there. I wish you well through this lesson," holding the frequency open for them. This does not suggest that you pump energy into them, although in certain situations you will most definitely want to produce energy to uplift the vi-brations of others. Do not mistake yourselves as messiahs. Indeed, you are here to vibrate and to change the foundation of human living; however, you are to inspire and to teach others to manage their frequency themselves, not to do it for them.

The Gods have battled over you for eons, changing their names, traveling from one reality to another. Today your Gods are movie stars, presidents, political leaders, and royalty. But who are they, and what do they really represent? When you look into their eyes, what do you see? The eyes of a truly switched-on human will hold a certain sparkle, a twinkle. The eyes of someone who has opened the energy doorways have a great depth and mystery, for the eyes are the windows to the soul, and yet they are more. They are your lens on the world, and those lenses are changing. Many situations that you thought were one way will shift overnight. Nothing is exactly as it appears to be and that is a truth, as truths go. Trust others but also use discernment, and apply your psychic abilities to assess all situations as you learn the power of healing. As you eradicate toxicity from your energy fields, you clean the ethers and attract other energy to yourselves, energy that vibrates with love. Like attracts like.

Today the use of deception is possible because you deny your psychic abilities. Deception draws deception. As human beings you are going to draw energies to you: your multidimensional selves, astrals, incarnates—all kinds of beings. Cultures throughout time have thought of the ancestors as spirits and intermediaries between the living and the dead, because they could feel their ancestors around them. Remember, they did not have modern-day media—motion pictures and television shows—to tell them what their visions should be. They created their own visions and saw their ancestors, those who had passed over; actually they looked for them. They believed that these spirits dwelt in trees and rocks and the Earth itself, which contained symbolic messages from the deceased. They also believed that how one died would indicate how one would live after death, and how one would return to life.

Surely this makes sense: The circumstances of your birth and their effect on you are beginning to unfold in a meaningful pattern. Everything that you experience is imprinted in you. Perhaps you have forgotten incidents in the early part of this life, just as you have forgotten other lifetimes, yet this knowledge is returning. As the importance of early memories becomes paramount for you to recall—where your ideas came from and who gave them to you—so too will the lines of time open. We want you to feel stable as the fan unfolds to the rest of existence, to what you are connected to. It is time for you to meet the Gods, not just to hear about them but to decide for yourself if the Gods and Goddesses from ancient times are real. Are they magicians? Do they understand how to manipulate reality so they appear to possess and merge with others?

You will discover that the symbols, tools, and codings that your ancestors left for you will have new meaning. The wave of genius and quickening of intelligence are happening very very rapidly. Trust this process. Be wise not to cement any one idea into reality today because ideas are bound to be shaken tomorrow. Build your foundation with your physical form, and then you will begin to understand what is happening in the heavens: what the comets are, what the great energy waves embody, who builds and flies the spaceships, and from what line of time they jump. Are Atlanteans jumping into their own future? Are earthlings from twenty-five years in the future coming back to change the Now?

The countdown during this fleeting moment of time is known by many. The World Management Team who currently influences your planet is composed of a cluster of families, a few thousand people in number. They rule the industries of banking, media, education, and the distribution of knowledge all over your globe, and it is they, a handful of people, who challenge your freedom. They are connected through their thoughts to other entities, just as you are. *The difference is they know it*, and you do not for the most part, so they use their tools and techniques to connect you to the entities that they wish to feed.

The idea of invisible vampires is not unknown. Remember, the Gods take all forms, and they come in to teach you and to fulfill their own destiny, which is to learn. How you learn and what lessons you attract in living will be determined by how quickly you learn the lessons in front of you right now. If the energy of the cosmos treats you to a great opportunity to love and forgive, and you do not take it, then you can be certain that you will have the opportunity to face that one again and again until you get it. And sometimes you will find yourself flat on your back, or perhaps flat broke, deflated, with no fizz in your mineral water, until you get it.

Master the lessons that are in front of you! Embrace the vastness of all living and trust that Family of Dark has its purpose just as Family of Light, and trust that everyone is part of both. All of your ancestors are related, and even if you came from different genetic experiments, you were made in God's own image, according to your old text. That, ideally, will give you a great clue about your genes, coupled with the discoveries that are being disclosed today about the ability to clone animals. Remember, once *anything* is cloned, everything can be cloned.

Choose to be healers; as you heal yourselves, your vibrations are felt and will inspire others to heal. The hidden mysteries and secrets that the ruling families of the World Management Team conceal need to be exposed and examined. Between now and 2012, all the cards will be put on the table, the secrets revealed. And these secrets, clues to multidimensional living, will be revealed for you to use them to heal. As humans you play out the same dramas as the Gods. When you fight here, you support the Gods fighting, and when you resolve and heal here, then you send that frequency to your ancestors of ancient Earth and of the heavens. You give them an opportunity to change their ever-expanding Now. Perhaps by seeding a valiant courage inside yourselves, you humans will inspire the Gods and they, with their power, will vibrate at a higher frequency from your inspiration!

Once again, breathe deep, give thanks, look around your life and know that everything is on time, in order, part of a plan within a plan within a plan. Wake up to it! Decide what you want for your part of the plan, and it will be integrated; then trust yourselves, be in the Now and heal.

Empire of the Mind

This fleeting moment of time, between 1987 and 2012, involves rediscovering ancient hidden ideas and examining what you have built your foundation on, and perhaps reorganizing it. Further consideration of how you have developed as a society and a culture may show that a great dismantling is necessary. We remind you to do the dismantling in your mind, allowing the old structures and belief systems, which are the core of modern-day political and educational thinking, to dissolve on their own. Without blame or anger, realize that you are in the midst of a perceptual shift. If you proceed in this way, the new energies will harmonize with your biological being; however, if you hold to ideas that are no longer vital and alive, you will find it very challenging to maintain your vitality and, we daresay, your life.

Changes of energies have a purpose. As we have said, everything has a frequency, and some frequencies are compatible and some incompatible with your being. Yet, the more you grow in consciousness and maintain the frequency of love, the more you will be able to transmute the incompatible frequencies into harmless energies. As you expand into the being that we are eliciting, you will have more energy, power, and love inside yourself, and the forms of toxicity outside you will have a free ride through your field. A higher vibration or frequency is created by the way in which you integrate and establish peace throughout your spiritual, emotional, mental, and physical bodies. Once this occurs, your frequency of self-assured, self-producing love and centeredness negates any harmful outside frequencies. Life is changing at an accelerating rate, and you are here to become winds of change, not to fight the change.

Perhaps you are reflecting on the words and ideas we pull through the dimensions to place on the buffet table for your nourishment. We ask you once again to consider what your life has been teaching you lately, what your body has been saying, what mirrors you have experienced, and how you have interacted with it all. And now that you know yourself a little more, ideally you can step back and, in your knowingness, release all judgments. If you feel that an area of your life needs attention, or if you find that you have slipped into patterns of experience or behavior you wish to avoid, then be aware of it. It is in these areas you will be tested to see if you can literally change your old behavioral responses.

Relax. There is no passing or failing these tests. You have done well to move this far on the journey of Earth in these times of momentous change, times which are sought out like hidden treasure. Explorers and divers on your planet travel the continents and oceans, following old maps and reading old legends, searching for buried treasure and artifacts of value, books of antiquity, or lost cities. Everyone has been in search of something. Earth is held in a similar regard, and it is this particular point in time that is a gem, a hidden treasure in the Book of Existence, and not merely Earth throughout all probable times. Gems of time are sought out because they hold something of unique value. You place value on material objects, and this has become such a focus of humankind that you have abdicated the power of thinking. Your institutions train you to become producers for a system that cannot produce enough, a system based on producing more and more, and throwing more and more away. As a result of giving your authority to others and believing what you have been told—rather than thinking for yourselves—you are overexpanding in the physical world, too focused on material comforts, and you have destroyed your environment, or so it appears. Rampant materialism separates you from the library of Earth found in Nature, which is your connection to the Mother.

As you expand your confidence and apply the new ideas springing forth in you, you will have many unique experiences. At first it may appear that you are alone in your expanded perspective, and if that is the case, it is important to feel good about it because self-realization happens alone, in the core of your being. If you are fortunate to be connected with other people from the beginning, then perhaps you will go through your isolation period later. However you are experiencing the discovery of who you are, it is important to grow from that point, allowing the fan of consciousness to unfold completely.

By now you have probably reflected on yourself, your bloodline, and your purpose for being, as well as the reason you continue to journey with us. In your reflection we ask you to go further while you read our words, to imagine yourselves into the past and the future, to journey both to the time of Atlantis and to December 2012. The infinity sign—the numeral 8—over your third eye can act as a transport center, so electrify and energize this symbol around your eyes, especially where the lines join at the third eye between the brows. Drift into this process and, seeing two vistas, find yourself in Atlantis and in 2012—for both places exist simultaneously. Remaining focused in the Now, notice your body, your breathing, and the energy around your physical form as we hold the doorway ajar—a window of time opened for you in both locations of time.

Coming from the year 2012, why would you return to this Now? And if you were from Atlantis, why would you choose this point in time? Holding these two avenues of time open in your mind and forgetting that you are from Earth, see if you can tune into why beings from other points of time want to enter into this fleeting moment. What would be the purpose? Breathe deeply and consider that the purpose these two groups of time-jumpers have in common is hunting treasure here. Polluted Earth, a treasure? What could the treasure be? This treasure is not so evident; treasures are usually hidden.

When you travel through the sites of antiquity on Earth, they appear to exist in your current reality, the year in which you visit them. However, in actuality all time exists in every moment, in every direction; even the place you are currently occupying has layers of other worlds and times only separated by their frequencies. It is frequency modulation that allows you to enter these worlds and times. Why do you think time-jumpers are coming to your world, what are they looking for? We daresay that they are here to affect your frequencies. An opportunity exists for all of existence to experience the frequency that you produce and the energy that you are, to participate in the unfolding within you of a unique version of reality where the closed fan can completely open in the blink of an eye.

The band of existence through which your science notes frequencies is called the electromagnetic spectrum. You exist as a frequency on that band, and like a radio signal you can be located; however your frequency is beginning to expand beyond that band, although the dial does not turn too far just yet. As the years unfold toward 2012, you will begin to gain full access to an expanded spectrum of frequencies, which is your destiny and why it is exciting to see what you will do with this opportunity.

We are time-jumpers who enter your reality and change

time; that is what some time-jumpers do. Your world exists like a piece of swiss cheese with holes permeating the field of existence, and Family of Light is here to mend some of the holes, those tears in the etheric fields where other energies have entered to wreak havoc with you. As third-dimensional beings you do not perceive the pollution your thoughts have created in the invisible realms.

For their own reasons, many forms of intelligence have come here to watch the version of your world that will unfold to a very high frequency, with you utilizing full-brain capacity and full access of the band of consciousness. Through the process of rapid and drastic accelerating change, some people will forget why they are here and will continue to believe scenarios of limitation. This lack of awareness is like a great mountain that you must move. How will you transmit the new energies so other people can feel the potential pathways? Many humans believe they are not capable of hacking their way into the new territory, and that is why Family of Light—time-jumpers extraordinaire, creators of change, rearrangers of systems of consciousness and of existence itself—is here to pioneer the new pathways of consciousness.

Once you discover the so-called harbors of consciousness, you must then move inland to the new territory inside yourself. You must become extremely focused on what occurs around you all of the time. Everything is a code, a message, and has many many meanings and many plans within plans. You are designed to expand into a much higher state of awareness, to move the tuning dial on the electromagnetic spectrum from where you have been located for eons, living in one little band of frequency. The energies of change and the shifts of consciousness propelled by cosmic forces have come to expand you, and as you expand you must consider many more possibilities. The new territory will be undecipherable at first, because you may journey into this new spectrum of opportunity and apply your old belief systems once you get there. Remember, many of the explorers who left the European continent five hundred years ago set out looking for one thing and found another. And when they made a discovery, they did not always understand it because they superimposed their old ideas and expectations onto the new world. The indigenous peoples who encountered the waves of explorers were hard-pressed to hold on to their connection to the great Mother Earth.

You can conceive of this expansion of your people that occurred five hundred years ago because you have studied it in school and know that the age of exploration has been extensive on this planet. Now it appears to many people that your world is full and that every nook, cranny, and crevice has been explored. Do not be fooled by this notion. The world is still a place of mystery, holding a multitude of territories that have barely been explored. You are like the drop of water that considers itself whole, yet is part of a great ocean. You have to expand to understand that you are connected to something massive . . . existence.

Earth's mysteries are pulsating and ready to unfold now, to share with you her own Book of Knowledge that holds many secrets. The core ideas you have studied in school about the age of Earth and the development of civilization will be discredited in the next ten years because a rapid acceleration of learning is occurring. Some of you may say, "Well, I have already thrown out my history books." We are speaking of a global expansion of consciousness and realization resulting from a few pioneers willing to reinterpret and make new roads of possibility into the realm of consciousness. Your co-humans will seek out the new roads because the ideas you pursue are fresh and vital and alive. Ideally, as the consciousness of Earth unfolds, you will interpret your role as that of significant beings.

As you establish balance within your own being, consider that everyone around you is coded to change. Those willing to be the pioneers will set the paths of frequency and make the highways and byways. Ideally, you will not all cluster together, yet will still realize that you are part of one gigantic possibility, where you are significant, where your value is priceless, and most of all, where you understand what value really means. The treasure is your ability to manifest yourselves as frequency beings, to span the electromagnetic spectrum, to live in it and to dance it as time-jumpers, understanding that you can change the frequency you hold in your being and that by changing it, you can access the worlds around you.

We remind you that it is essential for you to build strength and love in your physical being for the you who has an address and a name, the you who came through the birth canal of a mother. This is the you to whom we appeal, the one who is completely and totally ensconced, addressed, and located in 3-D. Whatever you are doing, you are part of the treasure, and if you are drawn to our words and to follow this journey, then rest assured that whatever you are dealing with in your life is helping you to unfold to that place of expansion where you will understand the laws of frequency. Perhaps the plants will teach you, or the animals, or you will become psychic with your family, friends, or your coworkers. You will begin to Know; your ancestors will unfold in you, and the possibilities that may seem vague and distant now will eventually become very real.

Sometimes you overfocus on "how" something will happen rather than putting your attention on "what" you want to occur. It is important for you to emphasize what you want. "I want to be well, I want to be creative, I want to meet more people and have more meaningful work. I want more abundance. I want to travel and explore the opportunities that exist in the world. I want love. I want new ideas." These statements set the direction for your arrows of intent, allowing the unfolding of multidimensional consciousness to be attracted to you according to the vibration in your field. It is essential for you to grasp that you are multidimensional creatures, and you will not travel the electromagnetic spectrum as yourselves, or not in the way you currently perceive yourselves.

Remember the explorers who went from a flat to a round worldview. They imposed their own paradigm on what they saw rather than allowing the indigenous people to teach them another worldview. Your ancestors did not always have a language for their multidimensional travels. There are no billboards and road signs, stoplights and rules of trafficking and travel; this is an unlicensed area, and no one is regulating or testing you to travel there. This is uncharted in your mind. Your ancestors had to build wooden sailing ships to traverse the oceans to discover the new world they were seeking, whereas you build ships in your mind, or ships appear that were built in the minds of others from Atlantis or 2012, seeking to explore the fleeting moment. What are the time-jumpers looking for? We daresay they are looking for you and what you can produce.

You are fascinating creatures; there is no doubt about it. You have a tendency to maintain and stick to what you find. Many of you are slow to change, and once you do change you hold on to your changes like a crab clasping with its claws—you hold that tight. It appears that if you can be stimulated to shift into a frequency that will change the way you experience the world, you will learn to maintain this frequency. This you can do; the challenge is in dismantling the old frequencies. Yet many of the cosmic weather changes coming your way are designed to assist you in this process. If the headline on a newspaper read, "Comet Here To Shift Consciousness," the statement itself would shift consciousness. You are so programmable that whatever you see in print you believe, for it is part of your nature to believe, which is why we appeal to you to have more discernment.

As your multidimensional self unfolds, you will be aware

of many time lines and places. You will contact the Ka energy or what we will call the *fiduciary*. The fiduciary will act in the capacity of a manager, as a multidimensional intelligence who conducts the flow of knowledge and energy into your being, watching so your circuits do not get jammed, so you can span the electromagnetic spectrum and keep your experiences in order. The fiduciary or administrator—also known as the higher self, and by some as the Guardian Angel—can facilitate your process of expansion. This intelligence has many names and takes on many shapes and is a part of your energetic field. Once you shift your frequency and build your vibration out-side yourself, you will begin to connect with these other forms of intelligence that are also you.

The fiduciary exists as a wayshower, as a travel guide be-tween sites of being and sites of existence. Most of you have traveled to parks, sacred sites, or recreational areas where you often find rangers and guides showing the way, pointing out the highlights and happenings of the area you are visit-ing. Well, imagine that there is an entity, an energy, a vast uni-fied collective voice that exists for each one of you as a focal point from where your expansion is managed, so you are not left fluttering in the winds of a hurricane, tossed around and tumbled upside down. The fiduciary, in actuality, can assist you in holding and moving your opening fan of conscious-ness, showing you which direction to turn and modulating the frequencies that contain events or vibrations that occur within a certain period of experience or time. Your personal name is part of your frequency; identifying yourself as human creates a frequency; your address, Social Security number, and everything used to relate to the outside world are part of your frequency, as well as whatever you say and think about yourself.

Some of you have become overfocused, repeating fre-quencies within your field by identifying again and again with the same life experiences, and as a result your fields of energy have become quite dull and devitalized. If you do not fill your energetic field with new experiences, new ideas, and new versions of yourself, your field becomes dim and worn, bored with the same old story. Once you have explored the depth of healing inside yourself and examined what you need to confront, move on. Create new stories. And when you tell the old ones, tell them a bit differently each time. If you repeat the same story about yourself again and again, then be aware that you are missing an opportunity to gather another perspective from those gems of experience: life or near-death imprinting memories, joys and ecstasies, tragedies and crises. When you speak of your experiences, intend to gain a new awareness, to hold a more expanded view, and to see what the story becomes. If you would each approach your lives in this manner, then when Earth relinquishes her hidden secrets, you will learn a different history about yourself as well.

The time-jumpers in general are not here for gold and artifacts, although a few want to discover books, to hide some things and to change others. Many are here to experience or affect your frequency, to modulate it in support of your expansion, while others seek to create chaos and confusion. The Earth knows these designs and is timed to perfection for her own unfolding. No matter how much weather control or destruction of the environment you wreak upon this great sphere of living consciousness, the Earth will still relinquish to you a greater story of yourself. Places where you originally thought civilization had sprung forth will be reconsidered. We mentioned that the Fertile Crescent was an area worthy of the Gods because there was plenty of water, the topography kept people separated, and it was easy to map. However there were other great waterways on your planet, and civilization always flourishes around the great waterways and rivers. As we look through the pages of time and see the probabilities that unfold, those of you who seek to understand your ancestors and the true meaning of living have already created a powerful force. The Earth feels this energy and will soon re-linquish antiquities and discoveries in the North American continent along the riverways that will shock the world. Flooding will wear away structures to reveal antiquities and show that the season of change is upon you.

In your day-to-day life, use common sense and respect because the years ahead will host a great play of Nature, where she will vie for your attention; just as the cable television stations and the Internet vie for your subscriptions, so too will Mother Nature. She will want you to sign up, to sub-scribe to her channel, which is free. So if she howls or rages outside your door, pay attention for she is calling to say, "I have a message for you. Change is here." And the change is not necessarily a change of neighborhood, a job, your mar-riage, or death appearing on your doorstep. The change is based on a frequency change within you: your habits, actions, and the way you participate in life. The fiduciary will link you up, becoming your own version of the Internet so that Mother Nature's vibrations and distribution of intelligence will be administered for you, and everything will make more sense. It is now possible for many of you to have this ener-getic linkup by building trust inside yourselves, knowing the link is there and never doubting it. You must build faith in the administrator, the fiduciary, for without that faith you cannot have the service.

As you perceive more it is important to understand that, although energies can appear in your field as solid beings, they may simply be riding the wave of frequency, matching frequency to frequency, appearing as real when they are merely holograms. You too can travel to places that appear to be real, yet your journey on the electromagnetic spectrum, fa-cilitated by the fiduciary, may be a holographic experience. You must explore the idea of holograms: What can be made? What can be developed? As with human cloning, holograms are nothing new. Everything your culture "discovers" in the years ahead is replication, repetition of what your ancestors throughout time could do. An artistry will spring forth, and you will wonder who planted the seeds, and where a garden this magnificent could have originated. This is a probability before you.

Look for that vibration and decide if you want to be in a renaissance of consciousness where you unfold and tap into the abilities that your ancestors held. And when you agree to participate, the Earth will reveal her layers of time to you. As we said earlier, where you sit right now, many worlds exist coupled and piled one upon the other, yet each is isolated and separate, full in its own integrity, unique and safe. How can so many dimensions of time share one space? How can so many lives and so many forms of intelligence all share one body and one mind? You may think of it as receiving five thousand television channels all at once, each with a different show. We remind you that the technology you are developing at a rapid rate and the secret technology hidden from you are both reflections of your own abilities. Remember as you move through the fan of time that everything can begin to splinter and fracture, resulting in too many pieces of uniqueness, like the frayed ends of a fabric, growing and growing until the fringe becomes longer than the great tapestry itself, dribbling off into a meaningless tangle of nothing. For this reason, it is essential that you keep yourselves woven together.

We have said often enough that you are here to learn to live, and that living will become a whole new experience. There is no reason to be frightened of the coming changes, although fear, fright, and hell on Earth will be expounded and sold in greater measure than ever. This twenty-five-year period is a test of how far you can go into forgetting and, in the same lifetime, bridging and reclaiming full memory. That may appear to you like Family of Dark forgetting, and Family of Light remembering. However, the World Management Team—considered by many to be Family of Dark—and the secret rulers of your planet seem to remember. They know about multidimensionals and that is the difference between you and them: They deal with the invisible realms because they have kept the secret knowledge for themselves.

Your Gods have disappeared in the Piscean Age, and it is Family of Light who has forgotten. So now you must remember what the Family of Dark knows, and come into balance with this knowledge, seeing the world you share with one another. You will be challenged to redefine what you consider light and dark, good and bad. On your own you may be baffled by this task, so keep your eyes open and see the connections made by your fiduciary. Listen very carefully to the voice of spirit, the Ka, that vague, ephemeral quality the Egyptians so valued. The voice of the fiduciary has its existence in many aspects of the electromagnetic spectrum, leading to many lines of time and probable worlds; this is an aspect of multidimensional existence that you are just beginning to access.

Picture your own administrator and imagine that a vast order of knowledge is being settled upon you now. We can assist in this energy transfer because it is a frequency we can broadcast, giving you the opportunity to vibrate with and hold it for yourselves. We send that frequency to you now, and it is your will and intent that will switch it on like a light again and again. Learn to use the administrator and feel the organization of intelligence that seeks you out, that calls you to know so much more, and leads you to explore third-dimensional living in such a way that magic unfolds before your eyes. The discovery of the clues to living and the Earth's true significance is not merely a journey for a few, or simply a career for archaeologists or staid members of explorer clubs. In this time it is the task for all of humanity to expand and explore.

As you contemplate your life and feel a change occurring inside, what frequency will you create for the Earth? What civilizations will you leave for your descendants to record? What legends and myths and feats of renown will they write about you? Remember, you have already been written about, backward and forward in time, and at this time you come back to this Now to gather more experience and to change. Our words may have you wondering about the continuity of time. If time can be entered at any moment from so many different directions, how stable is it? Time appears to you to be quite consistent and reliable. You just have to look in your history books to confirm time's stability. Yet, as you begin to unfold your fan, you will see that not only can you expand your consciousness into time, but all characters in time, who can find the right frequency and who desire to be pioneers and treasure hunters, can seek out the frequency band of Earth during this twenty-five-year period.

What is your job in all of this maneuvering? To let everyone jump in? To forget yourselves? Or are you ideally a treasure? Something truly profound springs from this nanosecond of existence that is currently just out of reach, yet on the cusp of revolutionizing human existence. Become aware of yourself as a valuable being, knowing that your every thought seeds the future. As Family of Light, we look in the Book of Earth and remind you that the frequency you are looking to build is one of love, and there are many ways to do it. Your ancestors did not always love the beings they met when their multidimensional selves unfolded, and they were often at war with them. The Gods came and filled the heavens with darkness and poisons; they also came and filled the heavens with sound and light and love. Your ancestral lineage on this planet, through the dimensions and through the heavens, is varied.

Energies are attracted here by your frequencies. Frequency seeks similar frequency. As Family of Light, you are here to create a frequency of healing and balance around Earth, to take the highest opportunity at hand, the most difficult task, and raise the frequency from one of despair and fear to one of great ecstasy, love, and achievement. Once this occurs and you have established Earth in this vibration, you will experience the thousand years of peace of which your stories and legends speak. You may think someone else is going to save you and create this peace—a Messiah, or ancestors from the heavens fixing your problems and giving you solutions to your illnesses and pollutions. In truth, the coming that you have been awaiting is the coming of consciousness. Again and again throughout the ages, a quickening occurs that offers the possibility to hold knowledge and to be responsible, to be a creator. There are some beings in the heavens who applaud you and see six billion new Gods potentially arising on Earth. What energy! What vitality! Six billion new Gods! Who will manage them? Will they weave themselves together or will they become frayed fabric, a tangled mess destroying themselves and going nowhere?

We share these metaphors and ideas with you as tales and imaginings, as stories that compel you to reflect upon your own living: why you live, why everything is so intense, and why every industry and every job is crumbling in some way. The newness that springs forth sometimes outgrows itself by the next afternoon, and brilliant ideas to make billions one day are seen as bankrupt the next. You are experiencing the expansion of human genius, and a fine line has always existed between genius and insanity. We want you to be clear about this! Genius/insanity, light/dark, yin/yang, good/evil are all two sides of the same coin. You may turn from one side to the other to know the fine balance between them, which is actually what you are seeking, the place where you know light and where you know dark. For by maintaining these frequencies, you support your connection to the whole with the same energy the Creator does, like a parent knowing that your children will all grow up and be fine.

The "real wholeness-frequency" is a feeling of peace within

yourself, a feeling of knowing your ancestors, knowing your past, present, and future lives and all of the probable lives you could have lived—you would recognize all the choices you did not make, and all those that were made and lived: the marriages, schools, jobs, travelings, and moves. Everything in your life is part of your multidimensional inheritance that the energy of the administrator, the Ka, can assist you to integrate. This energy is a voice of kindness, a voice that honors you, a part of yourself that assists the you who wants to state what you are and yet needs support in dealing with your development and growth.

The plan for Family of Light and for all those who care to come to the reunion of 2012 is to have a good time! Sometimes Family of Light plays the martyr role, as they did at the bridge of the Arian Age and Piscean Age and all through the Piscean Age where a tremendous number of martyrs appeared. Martyrdom is now over, and a playful respect for being human, with no offense to others, is your ticket to translate your vast multidimensional inheritance. Remember that you may not know at first where some of your abilities, ideas, and talents are derived from, yet truly a renaissance is upon you, and one so profound as to be recorded in the annals of time. You are watched to see what you will build as frequency modulators and designers of the mind. As you build the spans of your bridge into the next age, it is essential that you know who you are and what you want, and that you not be afraid of yourself as you encounter others—family, friends, lovers, and partners, and all of the various beings that occupy existence with you. Once again we remind you that this process of change is not designed to destabilize humankind: It is designed to rebuild the core of your beings, so you can truly become the magnificent beings your ancestors are awaiting.

You have been influenced by numerous forms of intelligence, and they will all return now—each of your influencers in one way or another—to combine their energies with you once again and to see what you will produce. Your influencers have taken human as well as multidimensional form. Beings of power that once walked your Earth—conquerors, kings, queens, popes, presidents, and other people of renown—are incarnated now to once again open their bags of magic tricks in order to live and learn a lesson. The Gods, and all creatures from the heavens taking various shapes and names, guises and disguises from angel to reptile, are all here in your world as they were in the world of your ancestors. Remember, the experiences your ancestors had with your multidimensional relatives could not be written, since often there were no words to describe what was occurring. To depict their experiences, your ancestors left signs and symbols, often carved in stone, as important information to pass on. Symbols help you understand abstract concepts based on direct experience that cannot always be translated into words.

As you expand in your ability to produce and experience various frequencies, the simple act of running your hand over any of the ancient symbols—stars, suns, moons, serpents, geometric shapes, squiggly lines, and dots—and of seeing them before your eyes will be enough to open the library doors where symbols will become whole lessons, like encyclopedias of knowledge based on frequency. When you emit your frequency while looking at these symbols, it can open an area of knowledge that your ancestors left to prepare you for at this time of opportunity and change.

You are unfolding rapidly now like a deck of cards endlessly fanned and rippled, and in every second of your existence you move quickly toward opening to more energy. Look around and be grateful for who you know; seek to learn from one another because it is through your relationship with each other that you qualify for relationships with your ancestors and the multidimensionals. You must remember that Earth is a treasure, sought out and hunted for on the lines of time, and you have something of immense value to offer, so be proud of who and what you are. A price-less quality is unfolding in you, so be alert to who you are and be grateful to be alive. The immensity of this task is al-most beyond description. It is as if you are journeying down a birth canal, squished and pressured to move from where you were comfortable, yet your will and desire to be alive push you out.

Many babies are not given that opportunity today. They no longer thrust themselves forward in natural birth, at least not in the Western world. Women have become fearful of the birthing process, and so their relationship to their intimate others, the babies they produce, has been compartmentalized and controlled. As women have become afraid of the experi-ence of birthing their own kind into being, the Goddess has been tricked into fearing her greatest ability: to bring forth and nurture life. We speak to men, women, and all of hu-mankind. Imagine who you can be. The thrust of birth that a child experiences is part of a natural movement into the world. When you unnecessarily cut children out of your bel-lies, you deny them their inherent right to thrust themselves into existence, and unwittingly hold a frequency of fear for them and who they might be, rather than a frequency of wel-coming grace no matter who they are.

It is essential for you to understand that as you explore your relationship to the world you populate and create, you must examine your method of reproduction. Cloning will not be a solution. The act of sexual intercourse imprints the cells and without it a certain vitality is lost, yet you may not dis-cover this difference for many years. You may eat genetically altered plants and animals and discover a long time from now that the vital substance was missing. Those who clone hu-mans, and have for a while, wonder why the clones are never quite up to snuff; it is because they were not created with the act of sex. It is true that humans can be born out of a violent sexual act; however there is still a vitality, a thrusting, a coming together with a passionate stir of energy, that imprints life—whether lovingly or violently. When life is stimulated by an electronic probe in a petri dish in a sterile laboratory, that life does not have the same vitality as the life that is true born.

People are having difficulty producing children these days. Sperm counts are down, and women suffer from nerves and anxiety over not living up to the icon of the Barbie doll. People no longer enjoy the sexual process. In some situations sex has become merely an act to produce children in order to get on with the business of buying things for them, then building bigger houses to hold their stuff, thus initiating children into a system that continues to destroy the Earth. Far too many humans have forgotten how to live as vital sexual beings. You have forgotten that it is essential to honor life, the life you produce and the life you live. We ask those of you who will be the creators of the coming generations to produce a frequency in your bodies that will establish a vibration of love, one that will open the lines of time to a whole new understanding of living. Invite the children you want to birth into your field. Guarantee them love as you call in the great keepers of love who are waiting to be born. Welcome your children and let them know that you are willing to learn from them as well about the vibration of love and how to produce it in unlimited abundance.

We appeal to you to populate Earth with people who maintain a very high vibration, and to do so means taking care of all children, not just the ones you personally birth. Start to really observe the children you encounter, and send a frequency that lets them know you are happy they are here. Today's children are all frequency projectors and modulators extraordinaire, and with each year new children are born gifted with greater ability to hold more and more frequencies. These children will not be satisfied with the worn-out ways and the old interpretations, so do not harm them by subjecting them to a system of medical care that works on fear rather than on healing. Your children often take on the difficulties you hold in your own field, especially those problems that you avoid. Pay special attention to what your children are telling you. Everything is symbolic.

The empire of the mind is vast, calling you from every continent and every direction. All of the Gods who left their footprints on Earth in all lines of time, those whose names are known and those who are unknown, all are returning. This is why many of you now feel impulsed to visit sacred sites, because the Gods held their events and staged their dramas at many of the ancient stone temple sites of your planet. When you visit these sites, you appear to be a third-dimensional Earth-traveler, while your other selves play out dramas in another time in the same space. Versions of yourself remember what else you have been, what sandals, shoes, or boots you wore on your feet, how you styled your hair and the color of your skin as you changed your human costumes, just as the Earth changes seasons again and again.

The heavens present an opportunity, so do not be afraid of what will appear. The light of comets and celestial bodies in various shapes, swirls, spirals, streaks, and flashes will punctuate the heavens, and you will not always be certain of what is transpiring. There are many means and ways in which celestial symbols and signatures can be produced, electronic and otherwise. In the late-twentieth-century Earth, you have invented devices with which to project images on the heavens, joining the time-jumpers arriving from Atlantis and 2012 as well as those who come from every direction of time, bringing their technology with them.

The show of existence is unfolding, and entities from everywhere bring their media equipment to park it here for this twenty-five-year period. And by now you are beginning to wonder how you will make sense of it all. How crazy will it become? It will become as crazy as you want. You will always have the opportunity to breathe slowly and deeply, to reflect on events, to put a smile on your face and say, "Oh, Great Fiduciary, thank you for assisting me, for keeping the threads woven together into a pattern I can decipher. When my ancestors opened to these realms and could not translate the experience into words, they brought their meaning into art. Allow me to also bring the meaning of this great change into my own version of a living art, an art that allows me to express the feeling in all of my being."

The making of great beauty is at hand, dear friends, a beauty embracing a rare essence of existence that we don't want any of you to miss. Become the creators of your own reality, six billion Gods awake, alive, and buzzing, and let the others wonder how to handle it! As you switch on and take charge of your lives, you will establish a whole new experience of living where, with your courage to be unique and pioneering, you will debunk fear and limited thinking. The Aquarian Age is an age where the Gods will be seen to be everywhere, in everything, more Gods than ever.

Family of Dark

As pioneers in consciousness, you are on a journey that can change course quite rapidly. One moment you can feel in balance, as if you are on top of the galactic center, and the next moment you can find yourself in one of the deepest and darkest black holes of existence. When you move into the realms of expanded consciousness, many tests are required of you, and this journey will take you into some dark, foreboding places as well. Many of you may want to stop before you enter the dark caverns, as if entering would guarantee self-destruction. We ask you to recognize that darkness is greatest before the dawn, and that the darkness holds many keys.

We address you as Family of Light—those who have forgotten their ancestral knowledge and are striving to remember. Your polar opposite, Family of Dark, remembers the invisible worlds and the teachings the ancestors passed down orally, or kept in secret texts and tablets, or carved in stone. Family of Dark has kept many secrets. In your mind the dark holds its secrets because you cannot see what is there. Explore the idea of opening your eyes in the dark and becoming comfortable with it, being able to see in the dark and therefore accepting it. Some of you are terrified of the darkness outside your door, or will not walk into an unlit room. You imagine all kinds of entities existing in the darkness. Your imagination is rich, and if it were equally as drawn to the light around the corner, you would accelerate your growth at a rapid rate. However, part of your psyche has a macabre fixation on the dark, both wanting it and feeling terrified of it at the same time.

We will now point out the path of darkness that has been prevalent in the Book of Earth, a darkness that holds secrets that would stop many from passing through it, a darkness that is itself an initiation. Yet there is a power there. We cannot call it a bad power, because power is power just like money is money, and technology is technology. Intention always focuses the use of knowledge, affecting what you create. As you journey further with us, the terrain becomes more mysterious and the shadows deepen, the crevices narrow and the sounds of unknown energies intensify. Imagine that you are walking by yourself into a dark, forbidden territory. Breathe deeply and tell yourself to relax, then call to mind some of the heroes of your planet, whether fictitious characters or living persons, who have faced challenges alone, met their own fears and moved through them. Let your heroes and heroines come to mind now, those who were pioneers in their own right, holding their own light as they bushwhacked their way through unique and unknown territory.

Whenever you go somewhere new, you are bound to meet an unknown. The presumptions you apply to the unknown territory determine what you will experience. You cannot go into a higher frequency of energy without exploring every territory; therefore the dark side of humanity and the dark side of existence now call to you to examine and understand them. The dark side of power has many secrets: hiding your inheritance as beings of biological magnificence, as well as knowledge concerning the power of your mind, the power to regenerate and replicate yourself, and to truly understand the processes of sexuality, birth, living, and death. You must learn to stop fearing the darkness, and to understand the wide variety of sexual expressions that create power, a power that rests at the core of your inheritance as human beings.

As your values change, you must recall the Divine Mother, the goddess energy, for it is she who is missing in the bonding of male and female. Her place must be rightfully restored within your stories of courage and living. The Goddess can be seen in both men and women, although for external representation it may be modeled as female. Female energy has taken many forms, sometimes appearing very controlled, designed to please those around her; and sometimes taking on a ferocious, warriorlike quality as in legends of the Amazons, the women who rode valiant steeds into war.

What is your current understanding of female energy? Historically speaking, the Goddess has been banished in the Piscean Age. It was not until almost the first five hundred years of this age that an agreement was reached honoring the mother of the savior, the one you call Christ, a focal point of this Piscean Age. The story of the mother and child is ancient and actually dates back thousands of years through cultures that knew that the mother held the power of blood. She alone could produce blood without wounds, and this was a dark magic. Blood holds the richness of everything you are, the sum total of your vibration; certain rituals of the Piscean Age even decreed the drinking of blood and the eating of the body. What do these words recall? You may say they are metaphorical; yet we say that everything is coded with a deeper meaning and that there is truth behind truth and plan behind plan. Truth is always based upon your ability to move from contraction to expansion, from degeneration to regeneration. So, to expand your point of view, consider the unthinkable, the completely and totally ridiculous. And understand that to become informed does not mean that you are converted.

Although energies can be created through the power of sex, you experience sexuality for many different reasons. For most of you, there seems to be a drive; you say your hormones are alive, and you seek a partner to create a release and exchange of energy. You receive pleasure, get what you want, and move about your business. You often do not associate what happens on a biological, cellular level with the sexual act. The act of sexual intercourse is a regenerative force, and the orgasmic experience can be used to enhance and build a much stronger energy field. However, the expression of sexuality can also produce something entirely different. When sex is not based on love but is used for ritual abuse violation, many other possibilities can occur.

Some ancient cultures on your planet, especially in the East, were wary of sexual relationships during eclipses, and new and full moons. They understood that the energies of the heavens influenced your field of energy, which connects you to the etheric realms. They also understood that the astral realms were a place where beings can become trapped. We daresay that Earth is now permeated with lost and fragmented beings seeking wholeness, who have collapsed into your energy fields. Your fear of living attracts these astral entities, and then you make a home for them. They are often humans whose spirits were fragmented by dying, their fields shattered because they did not know how to die or even realize they did. You have been steered toward fearful deaths through stories that do not unite you with who you are, and so you die poisoned—sick and toxic. It is difficult to rise up like a fountain and keep yourself intact when you approach the great doorway of death in this state. This is a vast problem on your planet. These astral beings are like parasites that are attracted to you. The astral realms continue to collapse and pour down onto you humans; you then become possessed by these energies, and although you do not recognize their presence, your lives change. You may feel drained and depleted, or your habits suddenly become bizarre, and you cannot sleep at night, have headaches and unexplained body aches and illnesses. In actuality, you are battling more than a toxic Earth where foods are irradiated, or grown outside your country and then returned full of poisons.

The minds of people are unsettled and becoming so readable that the airways themselves are no longer peaceful, and as you become more psychic, you will feel the restlessness. Fear is always used to divide and conquer people, and *divided and conquered you have been throughout time*. That is another test of this era. Will you gather the great oncoming energy and weave yourselves back together? Or will you splinter and create more wars and separations? There are energies that want you separated on the physical level and on the interdimensional planes. Vast beings, living for thousands of years in your terms, make their living ruling and parenting you, seeking their value from you because you have considered yourselves valueless and purposeless. Those who would rule you on the physical and multidimensional planes understand the power of your genitals to create life, pleasure, pain, and death. They use your genitals as doorways without you even realizing it. And now the minds of your children are slowly being influenced so that their innocence is siphoned off in an invisible fashion, and this too you do not even notice. It does not serve for you to be angry and to blame other people for what is occurring, for these are signs of the times. If the innocence of the children has been lost, then look to yourselves and see what you have done to allow it.

The mother and the child story that exists all over the planet is an important one for you to remember. Symbols speak of more than what is evident. In these stories, where is the father? In this day of cloning and new methods of reproducing yourselves, many people will want to regenerate themselves through technologies, through acquiring body parts, and through surgeries—plastic and otherwise. A tremendous misuse of power occurs with human embryos that are procured on your planet, as well as with people of all ages who disappear. Some leave the planet and others go underground; a huge market exists in the selling of people on your globe. How will you change this? First, you must learn to value the life that you produce from your sexual coupling, because if you do not value that life, it may not create its own value.

Wayshowers are repatterning many realities now. They live quietly, and you may never hear their names, yet they are pioneering new avenues of frequency where the dark conspiracy stories of planetary, solar, and galactic control can be understood. This is no mystery to those of you who have spotted the clues over the years, the synchronicities that have shown you a bigger picture of existence, where everything is much more connected. Yet you have been encouraged to believe that nothing is connected. To understand the restructuring of Earth's frequency, you must first learn about the controllers of Earth because the challenges you will be facing in the next fifteen years will involve the darkest of the dark energies, the darkness before the dawn. Some of you will eventually ask, "How could things have become so corrupt?" Well, how could they? That is for you to answer. Your challenge is to go from the lowest of frequencies to the highest, and exploring the dark misuse of power will take you there.

You are regridding Earth and changing the frequency so that one-by-one lights go on and fields of energy are established. You must learn how to stop feeding those vampires who suck your energies, from the astral planes, from the dimensions, and from on and under the Earth herself. Your sexuality and how it is used are the key elements. Many leaders from around the globe, particularly in the fields of politics, religion, and education—especially in those areas that are purportedly dedicated to children—are part of a massive covert organization of pedophiles who use children for sex. This can occur when parents are not in communication with or in touch with the children themselves. It can occur because this inclination is passed from one family member to another for generations. This is one of the darkest secrets of Family of Dark on your planet. The houses of the rich are riddled with this secret: sex with family members, sex for ritual abuse, sex for calling-in darkness and the dark Goddess, where no vibration of love exists, only a vibration of seeking power.

When we talk about power and darkness, do not feel that you have to run away from this realization to have light. You must learn about the power of darkness in order to understand the wounds and waywardness in the souls of these beings, who are desperately seeking something that was never given to them by their parents or by anyone else. Because of this lack the practice stays in their bloodline. What is missing? You already know: It is love. The wayward ones on your planet, whether murderers, rapists, pedophiles, or mass manipulators, are all devoid of love and do not know it. And so your task of healing the planet will grow greater as the dark secrets of the world's ruling families and their dark occult practices are discovered.

As we look at the Book of Earth, we see that in so many cases your ancestors made the same mistakes. They wanted the pomp and circumstance of the royalty that paraded before them, especially when their own celebrations and festivals lost their meaning, when the cycles of time and the meaning of light and dark—the modulation of cyclical change—were lost and they became fixated on an outside world. You gave your power away to leaders who in many ways felt obligated to assume the power that you pressed on them; they did not know how to generate it themselves. Their fathers and mothers and grandparents were introduced to mysteries and practices, which often began benevolently. It may be the same for you as well. However, *on the path to power, when darkness crosses your path, you cannot run from it.* For many of these rulers—who at one time were benevolent powerful beings—when darkness crossed their path, they made an alliance. They took on power over others through secrecies and lies, and since one lie creates another and another, honesty became harder and harder to maintain.

Misuse of sexuality is not new. Child pornography and child slavery, the slavery of men and women around the globe, and the raping of men and women, have always been common. You have hidden the practice in your stories of Earth and do not study the subject in your classrooms. Perhaps you will consider studying the dark, having a course in your schools devoted to the dark misuse of power. As you educate your young, it is important to place the cards of darkness on the table. In many areas around the world, the dark forces are acknowledged and offerings are made, tokens left. Even in the practice of exorcising entities attached to humans, an offering of food or a piece of sweets is used to pull the entity into the offering.

You relinquish your history, your story of the richness of living, and trade this off for meaningless texts that require you to produce meaningless data so you can continue to live meaningless lives. You attend family reunions, picnics, and cocktail parties, assuring each other that you will continue to make your mortgage payments and be good citizens. You drink and eat your society's poisons and turn your children over to a Big-Brother, mind-control World Management Team where one does not think but simply performs at warp speed, or is eliminated. Newspapers, television networks, and the media are all owned and operated by a small handful of individuals. True ownership of these enterprises is difficult to track because there are plans within plans and players behind players, and nothing is exactly as it appears. It is time to wake up and realize that you are being fed information designed to limit and control you, to have you support and become part of the economy of death. As you lose your vitality you run from one so-called medical person to another, using up your insurance, your inheritance, to guarantee what? The sicker you become and the more you search, the more you keep this economy of death thriving. Do you understand?

As we share the dark part of the story with you, such as the covert and perverted sexual practices of your rulers, it is not for us to name names. You will discover for yourself that, in every country around the globe, those in the highest of positions have been put there because they are qualified by their perversions to hold power over others. This has been a secret for eons, but today everyone is coming out of the closet, so to speak. Mayors are cross-dressing in public, and pretty soon you will have a president or a pope cavorting as a chorus girl. Everything has gone topsy-turvy, and no one is certain of what is what any more. Your values are all askew and rightfully so. It makes a good starting place. As you examine the dark misuse of humanity and how you have been tricked, scammed, and schemed against, perhaps you will throw out all the frivolous adornments and reestablish a value for yourselves based on your power as spiritual biological beings. Ideally this is the probability you will choose as the threads of change wind and weave themselves through late-twentieth- and early-twenty-first-century Earth.

Angry protests will arise from people around the globe, and the energies will intensify to an outrageous state, energies that ask you to change. There will be shocks and scandals the likes of which you have never seen. Ideally you will wake up and see that what is happening in one country is happening everywhere. In another age the people were once divided by the Tower of Babel, when the Gods came down and said, "These people are unifying and pretty soon they will be greater than we are. Let us confound their tongues and divide them." And so the diverse languages were created. Today few of you are bilingual or trilingual. Mostly you are isolated and compartmentalized in your own little houses, unconnected to your neighbors or to the globe you live upon; yet you claim to be a global community, alive through electronics, as if the longevity of the globe, alive for billions of years, does not register. Remarkable.

We ask you to rethink and reevaluate your lives as you are called to regenerate yourselves. You shall change, you will change, you must change, because it is the season of change. When the storms become dark, find your courage and face your fears. Ask for assistance from your great trustee, the fiduciary, who will help you find the dark and survive the encounter. When you run from the dark you give it more power, allowing it to perpetuate itself. When you ignore practices that harm others, especially those of a sexual nature, then you uphold the act of harm. Each of you is called upon to heal the human spirit, to make a frequency on Earth where newborn babes, who will bring in the frequency of love, are valued and loved in return. You must guarantee that your young will not be violated, turned into mind-controlled zombies or sex slaves, shipped to other planets to work on farms, become genetic laboratories for body parts, or produce their young for questing multidimensionals desperate to rebuild their own depleted genetics.

Many indigenous people of your world were in touch with their multidimensional ancestors. They knew them through the dimensions, through time, and through their own blood. They also knew that they would live again and again, which is why in the development of their own cultures they planned ahead, sometimes for seven generations. Your ancestors understood this principle, which has been deleted from your sacred texts. However the World Management Team remembers. Family of Light and Family of Dark do not have separate books of knowledge. They can each know the same information. In the near future people will track their lineage in a different way. Today you track family trees based on parents and grandparents, yet soon you will structure yourself from a multidimensional lineage. At first there will be many imposters as there often are when the gates open to new territory. You may find wild, rabble-rousing multidimensionals who live free—yet rarely with integrity—claiming to be your kin. You must learn to recognize when you are fleeced or had, taken or stung. Do not hold anger over your realization; simply wise up!

Your world leaders have been acting this way for centuries. Today there is a tendency to play with the dark in a way that is more audacious than ever. Why? It seems in the Book of Earth that, without Family of Dark outrageously, preposterously trashing every single one of your values and boundaries, you would never awaken. You would remain complacent, like cows chewing cuds, never noticing what was transpiring. So the outrage, the insult, the shock, the distressing misuse of trust, will wave their banners high on Earth. When it reaches that stage, you can say to yourself, "Ah, the time is at hand." And once that stage is reached, know there is still much more to come. No humans live long enough or are quite clever enough to come up with these immense plans of control, so when you look behind the scenes, you will learn about an ancient race with their own tale of division, a tale of secrecy and hidden power. They are the ancient reptiles, your ancestors, your kin.

Reptilian beings have been ruling behind the scenes for eons, placing puppets in front of you as their messengers. These puppets often do not understand that they are possessed and taken over by the massive manipulators. Sometimes, when they do discover that they are part of so immense and grotesque a plan, they feel shrunken and shriveled even though they may be popes, presidents, kings, queens, or others of prestige and power. They recognize that they are nothing more than mere tools, taken over because they made a home for these forces through perversions, lies, their attachment to sex, and their lust for material objects. Your world is full of darkness, a different version today as versions go, but no different in its impact than the lessons that the darkness assists you to learn in all ages.

It is one thing to read about outrageous scenarios in newspapers and quite another to have them fall into your lap. Wherever the darkness finds you in your life, know that it comes in through difficult situations where your fear may rise like a wave of energy running up your arms, electrifying the stem of your brain, the reptilian brain, asking you to remember something. When this happens, know in the core of your being that you are part of a plan, and that your chapter is now ready to unfold into the deepest part of darkness so that you can create change by changing your frequency. You cannot reach the light without knowing the dark, and the dark comes now in massive amounts asking to be healed. There will be a tremendous exposure of shocking perversions because love from mother to child and father to child is missing. The form of love we speak of has not been practiced here for hundreds of thousands of years. Genetically you are dealing with the cleansing of a long long line of humanity, generation upon generation of wounds.

It is a challenging time in which you live, a challenge to examine how degenerate humankind's frequencies have become as a whole. The task ahead is to not underestimate the job, but to truly look at the darkness and see the work that has been cut out for you: to regenerate yourselves and your planet by finding what is really important, what you are going to value. Shocking changes will create a destabilization of civilization, and this is all meant to be. Some of you want to experience the time of light as if you were driving from one picnic to another. That is not the case. The issue of accountability must be addressed on your planet; not to blame people but to teach them that at this time each person must be his or her own leader. The truth is that no one is going to lead you. You are coming in to the Age of Aquarius where the Gods become visible, where everyone is a God.

Do not become frightened when your leaders fall. It is all designed so you can know the worst of family secrets: that parents sexually abuse their children from generation to generation because they do not know love. Love must prevail. You must clean your biological line, the ethers and the astral plane, because the new children wanting to be born will only be attracted by a frequency that guarantees they will be cherished. Without the cherishing of your children, you do not guarantee the continuity of humankind on Earth. This also requires that you respect and cherish the sexual act, for the quality of your couplings will determine the frequency in your energy fields. There is no escaping this truth: Your sexuality happens to be the seat of your biological power. It is through sexuality that you arrive here, and even though cloning is in vogue, if you were to jump into the future, you would see that you cannot create a clone of yourself that is as vital as you are. As we said, clones are not imprinted with the vitality of sex, with the experience of living beings, and so they fall short of expectation after a while. There are many cloned humans in your world as well as many designed doubles. This practice has been in place for thousands of years; it was initiated to replace those in power by look-alikes. Today the art and science of cloning is more fine-tuned, an art learned from multidimensionals who have lost their procreative power and have come here to secretly steal yours. However, those with true power need no secrets. True power is yours, and it can be shared or given away again and again. In the giving, it simply increases, and by holding on to secrecy and hiding it, power eventually diminishes and shrinks.

Accept your power by accepting the stories of darkness, knowing that your ancestors faced the same challenges, although not as magnanimously as you. You have so much assistance. The fiduciary is there to weave you through a massive expansion of power, an understanding of yourself that is so complete, so complex and awesome, that it is as if you were growing from a seedling to a giant sequoia in an afternoon! Contemplate that. This acceleration of beauty and power is the inheritance today's energies call forth from within you as you pass through new territories of awareness to grow to the light that you so desire to be, the light that touches each and every one of you. Light too must be understood; for the Gods play their tricks, you know, even with light.

The solutions you seek will be found inside yourself. Your feelings about and responses to the shattering world around you require you to rebuild yourself by accepting what is taking place; for in dissolution something new is created. The life cycle includes death followed by new birth like the story of the phoenix rising out of the ashes. This understanding is an important phase of your development, and the solution is for you to weave together and make sense of the multidimensional perspective you are learning. Make peace and gather with your loved ones and friends, honor and respect each one, violate no one's territory, whether through word, action, or deed. Honor all as you would be honored and understand that the great wounds of the human psyche come forward now, wounds that are a legacy in your genes, wounds passed on as darkness. The wounds of the ancestors will now be brought to the light of day, and it will appear that the task of healing is beyond you, that you have no salves or antibiotics for the diseases of the mind that will be revealed. These diseases or discomforts have been invisible for a long time. As you search to discover their cures, do not forget that you are multidimensional creatures and often the solutions lie not just in the physical body but in the astral planes, those invisible worlds where beings are attached to you, where possession and merging occur like night and day.

It is to this area of spirit that you are called, and when the darkness is the greatest before the dawn, know it is a spiritual clue, so open your eyes and do not be shaken by the hooting owls and strange sounds you hear in the night. Go forward into the territory of the dark and hold a lit candle to see what is there, intend to understand it, then open your heart and know that the diseased mind within the human spirit is waiting to be healed. The dis-ease of the mind separates you from one another, creating violence between lovers, families, and friends. It is a dark violence that cloaks itself in secrets and controls the spirit in a way finer than any mind control your 3-D operators can ever hope to achieve. The mind controllers and those who influence the weather and all aspects of your economy, religion, education, and medicine will be revealed because you are now ready to take charge and influence yourselves. Only by understanding how you have been influenced would you then dare to be in charge. As humans you have so abdicated the power of living that you do not know you are walking zombies.

Those responsible for your plight think they are so much better than you; however their darkness creates endless difficulties for them. You must begin to heal these wounds. Your compassion and forgiveness must include an understanding of existence on a scale broader than any apparent singular 3-D events, a realization that these misuses of power are predominant throughout the pages of the Book of Earth. The healing must be deep. In this process you will find your power and ideally heal your wounded leaders, and wounded they are indeed. Some will self-heal, others will proclaim their shame and, once they have exposed their darkness, become great leaders. However most will create their own destruction, and you will have to clear the astral planes of their polluted forms.

You will need to call out to the people, to those who have kept their old traditions alive, sharing the teachings of the ancestors, the ways of the mysteries and of the spirit world, the importance of balancing the light and the dark, the importance of the four directions, the elements, and the cleansing rituals and practices that have been left to you. This is one of the greatest challenges you now face: how to negotiate with and claim your power from beings you cannot see, beings who have far more power than you ever realized. So it is the reptiles who are in need of healing in order to reestablish the frequency of love as the foundation of their existence. We are not saying that all reptilian energies are rampantly moving toward evil, just as it would be unfair to say the same for all humans, although it could appear that way if one were uninformed about either group. We know there are many good humans, and it is time for them to awaken because they are encoded to develop the tests of their own power.

As Pleiadian travelers and time-jumpers who seek to know and explore ourselves, we have certainly looked into the dark dark chapters of the bigger Book of Existence, and we have seen these tests again and again. They are different in every place, and yet they are all the same. The perversity, the charge of energy received from harming others, is what keeps you separated. Usually your body's sensing systems and the mechanisms for accessing higher, lighter, and ecstatic frequencies are closed down, nailed shut with "no trespassing" signs. The beings who feed off harm to others, whether they are humans or multidimensionals, are feeding their energy fields through a limited channel, and this energy is not freely flowing through them. So when they access energy, they want a lot of it and usually of a violent nature. Those who create harm to others are starved energetically. Why? Because they do not have love and do not feel connected and are shut off from living. The walking living dead is what you are without love.

These are not gratifying concepts to hear about yourselves as humankind, yet we do not say them or share them in judgment. We see Earth and her cycles as flows of energy. Our intention is to let you know who you are, to mirror for you, and to document the quest that you as humankind have undertaken. When you are climbing a mountain, it is a very different experience than when you are on a plain looking back. Climbing creates a possibility to evaluate the terrain from one point, then reevaluate it from another. You are now living in the swamplands of Earth. There are joyous places to visit and exquisite times to be had; however the swamplands cannot be missed. The dank, dark energy must be acknowledged, then you can decide to do with the swamps what you will. The ancient Gods drained the swamps of Mesopotamia and created fertile lands.

Numerous creative choices call you; however the focus of healing is most important for you to embrace at this time. Massive unrest will lead to revolutions, uprisings, cries of vengeance, and anarchy, and many leaders will flee their lands. This in itself is a sign. The people will find their voice. The United States has a destiny, as does each country on every continent. At whatever corner of the world you find yourself, with whatever blood is running through your veins, find your dignity and be proud to be human. You must link yourselves as a collective of human beings; it is the pride you could feel about being a human from the planet Earth that is missing from your collective life. We do not refer to an arrogant pride but one that opens your hearts and connects you to oneness; in doing so you add the qualities of significance and purpose to your lineage and to your chapter in the Book of Earth.

Energies of different shapes and sizes come through the heavens, although the reptiles appear to hold your biggest challenges because they are behind-the-scenes rulers. They are particularly dominant in the World Management Team and other structures that you revere, especially those of a religious nature. They encourage their participants to follow meaningless rituals and to teach others to do the same. If you participate in a ritual, make it your own or be certain that you understand what is occurring. It is easy to siphon off your power, to have you say your hallelujahs, amens, and prayers without you really understanding who or what you are invoking. World religions will fall in the same way that history books will be thrown out.

Unusual sightings in the heavens will continue—streaks and balls of light, comets, mysterious fires in the skies, unusual lightning, and bizarre phenomena. We remind you once again that without the dark you would not see this play of light. The cosmic frequencies involve many layers of plans. You may ask, "Are these sightings natural occurrences or artificial?" The Creator is in everything, so is anything natural? Is anything artificial? Is it not all connected? Frequency control of your mind will become a paramount issue of concern on your planet: how you are given visions through television, computers, music, movies, and through invisible microwave transmissions that influence your thought patterns and your patterns for living. Mind control will be seen as the ultimate battle with darkness.

As your world leaders show their wounds and tell their stories and you see similar patterns from country to country, you will ask, "How could this be?" The darkness will grow and you will eventually see the 3-D plan to design and program human thought, to separate compartments of your mind, as if you were to name each cell of your body, making each cell a different individual. Those who plan to control your frequency would have all of those cells unconnected to each other, living together and never realizing their separateness, unaware of a connection. Because you separate yourself from your children, from the power of your genitals, from one another, and from wanting to know your power, you provide a fertile ground for the compartmentalization of your mind. Mind control is not new. Frequency control is perhaps a new term; however mind control has been around a long time. As you explore the ways your minds are controlled through overt and covert operations in your world, you will eventually understand the control that comes through the dimensions: what power, what occult inheritance and legacy you really battle.

The books of the ancients will have greater meaning if you do not presuppose their message. These books mention arrivals from the heavens and hold many clues as to what you will face. Uncovering the dark in all its awesome power will herald for you the power of the Gods. It will be one thing to face the perverse practices and mind control of your world leaders and to take a stand and demand integrity, yet at the same time to love and have compassion for that which you would really want to destroy. However it will be quite another thing indeed for you to stand back—like the story of David before the giant Goliath—when you begin to understand the entities that these very wounded world leaders really represent. All those in exalted positions will find themselves playing out leadership roles to the masses so that you will each claim your own power.

Teachings from the dark side show you the traps to avoid with your inheritance of power. With this quickening those people willing to be exposed at this time are on their own stage, mirroring for the world a new teaching, especially those who receive tremendous attention. No one is ever a victim, although your conquerors would have you believe in your own victimhood. How else could they conquer you? In the biggest Book of Existence and in the Book of Earth, there are no victims, only those who forget they are creators and who choose fear, forget love, and separate themselves. It is the same story with different players, again and again. Actually, in the broader picture it is the same story with the *same* players again and again.

We ask you, with the courage of your being, to call forth the darkness that is waiting to be healed. From a place of love and a place of courage, as Family of Light we ask you to send out a call and say, "Darkness, misuse of power, violation and perversion of peoples and the Earth herself, it's time for you to reveal yourselves. And in the revealing will be a healing. So come forward Dark, that the world may know you, and then we may know the Light and all rejoice as one." This is a noble call and does not imply that darkness will take over your life. You are calling for darkness and misuse of energy to be healed so that all humans can express their sexuality with love, so that children are honored and given a rightful opportunity to initiate their own sexual explorations without having sex forced upon them through ritual rape and violation.

It is in this very deep part of your regenerative self, your sexual organs, the core of your being, that many of the main problems lie, problems so dark, so secret that no one would dare speak of them. Yet they must be revealed. To relinquish power over your sexual organs is truly to abdicate the power of living. By *power* we mean a sense of connectedness and accountability, the maturity to know when to express yourself sexually and when not to, to know that sex is a consensual act in its highest form, and that the creation of life must be consensual. This is why your cloning will never work; it is not a consensual act, and spirit is not factored into the process. You are unique biological human beings and, as we have said, the Gods stashed their stuff in you, the best of everything. It is light extraordinaire that you create. And by cherishing your genitals, your biological substance, and healing yourselves, the potentials inside you are activated.

So we ask you once again to look at your life. What have you done to make peace, to find a purpose, to throw out what you do not need, and to release judgment of what you have done? As ancestors, as multidimensionals, and as humans in this and other lifetimes, what have you learned? Establish a value that will see you through the next stages of expansion and those of pulling together, synthesizing everything you are and coming to an integrated, exalted place of living. First you must make peace with the sexual organs of your being because it is here that life springs forth. You can be a pure well-spring for life, whether you have children or not, for your vibration acts as a source of life, and you are challenged now to maintain it. By valuing your sexuality, you can perhaps reestablish the frequency of humankind and qualify to bring in the new children, who must be guaranteed that they will be cherished as the ultimate resource of humankind. If only each of you had been given that guarantee, born as an ultimate resource! Sometimes what you do not receive yourself is the gift you give as your own legacy.

Raise your vibration at this time from the core of your sexual self, from how you identify yourself as male or female, and imagine that your being finds a stance and grows in value. Give up your confusion. Seek that which values you. Lay down perversion and distortion and all that harms the vibration of human dignity. For those who confuse you, recognize that their confusion is theirs and your clarity is yours. The confusion will become greater as men appear as women and women appear as men, all convinced that these are androgynous times. It seems to us, as we look at you, that you are seeking balance inside yourselves and that you are what you are, and yet nothing is exactly as it appears to be. Seek wholeness, seek health, seek sane living, seek to understand the dark and ask the fiduciary to be your trusted administrator, to guide you through the way ahead. And most of all, seek to understand the power of your sexuality, to infuse its expression only with love, for sex without love is truly not worth experiencing. Each of you must come to that conclusion and hold a standard; then perhaps you will create a new population for Earth, a whole new legacy as you bring dignity to the act of creation.

Your creativity ends when you are in fear, and your power ends where your fear begins. There are many fearful experiences that you must face, for you must know the power that fear holds over you and let that power become your own so that you would wield it in a gentle way, taking one thing and turning it into another—being alchemists and shape-shifters. This task is enormous as you move from the late-twentieth- to the early-twenty-first century, yet the probability of success is there. In the Book of Earth, the lines of time are not erased; they are there and you can find them, so seek them out. When you go to sleep at night, use the power of your will and intent to travel in your dreams. When you look around your community, at your family and friends, know that all are going through this test; perhaps they do not express it the same way, but all of you are experiencing the same intensity of living, so find what you have in common, and seek love.

The Gift the Gods Await

Throughout the course of our journey with you, we have made mention time and again of the ambiguous group of beings called the ancestors, who, as you have learned, exist in all directions: through time, through the bloodline, and through dimensions as well. Your ancestral lineage is not only comprised of your predecessors; you actually burst outward like a sun with many rays, touching multiple realities, and this is part of the expansion of consciousness you are now experiencing. The spirit world is vast and untold numbers of beings can approach you through the invisible domains.

In the Piscean Age, the spiritual world was thought to be invisible, which does not mean it was nonexistent, for your ancestors all experienced this force, although each perhaps in a different way. Now, without miracles, mysteries, and secrets, focus on the electromagnetic spectrum, your interpretation of light frequencies. Imagine yourself right now expanding and shifting along its entire spectrum, as your ancestors did, jumping from one point to another. The expansion of consciousness you seek calls you to shift to a frequency similar to the mysterious beings of the invisible world.

Perhaps when you learn where certain beings are located on the frequency bands and you can dial them up, then you will rename and readdress the whole idea of religion on your planet.

Your ancestors were not always able to express in words their experience of jumping from a 3-D perspective into other frequencies and then returning, or that entities from other parts of the spectrum could jump into their reality. It happens both ways. Old manuscripts, certainly the book you call the Bible and various disputed texts never shown to the public, hold mysterious references and enigmatic tales of interventions from a time long past, of events that are inexplicable from your current worldview. Though speculated about for eons, the events were not directly experienced by your historians; therefore those who charted the history began to create their own interpretations in order to understand the invisible world of spirit.

You are now challenged to look at your founding philosophies and educational belief systems, and to generously consider that the interpreters of these experiences did their very best. However, on one level the World Management Team now controls the flow of information to your world, so if you really want to know the truth, you must dig deeper and move around "politically correct" belief systems, questioning your own trust in the institutions of so-called higher knowledge. Religions have always attempted to control people by explaining the inexplicable to the masses, and as we look at the Book of Earth, we see that you have needed this assurance. You like mentors and teachers, someone to take you under their wing, whom you can turn to in your innocence, inquiring about the higher mind and spirit, the great mysteries and what the impeccable walkers of the spirit world understood. Actually you are gifted with a mentor, so we ask you once again to consider the fiduciary, the one who will serve your interests and show you the way—the one you can trust.

As you expand your perceptions beyond the flat-world consciousness, you will have to reconsider all of your beliefs; and even those of you who have already reconsidered so much of reality, you too will be asked to go further. You are all called now into the home of spirit, the house where mysteries reside and are held in trust as part of your great inheritance. You will soon discover that this invisible realm is indeed visible. As you experience your lessons in living, trust that events you would not ordinarily book for yourself are written in for you by the fiduciary, sometimes taking you through the times of sudden, shocking, and surprising changes to face what you would seemingly never choose. Based on your greater understanding of the purpose of living, you will now realize that you do choose what you encounter in order to pioneer a new way of being.

To have journeyed this far with us, you must consider yourself a pioneer. Even though there are six billion Gods now awakening, the process first happens to a few and then, like the sun's rays spreading over the Earth, the energy imbues everyone. It is time to climb upward now, to head toward the peaks of your own existence, where you already know that your destiny is to live, experience, and discover that spirit has not forgotten you. Life is significant if you would just notice. A massively alive intelligence surrounds you in the ether, and encourages you to go further and further on this journey. Once you have acknowledged the swamplands of difficulty and faced your fears, a very high peak appears in the distance, a majestic mountain beckoning you forward. If you wonder how you will ever reach this exalted peak, it will be with one step at a time. You have traversed the swampland and discovered the dark territories that held what you feared and thought you could not face, and by now you have ideally found that it was not so terrible. The lesson in traveling through the dark lands is that the light of faith sustains you, and now you have the opportunity to climb the great mountain ahead that offers, at its peak, a grander vista of understanding.

Imagine six billion human Gods awakening, all with ancestors most certainly connected to you, as if you were the center of a wheel with many spokes. Everything in life is significantly connected. The mountain that beckons you to climb its peak, you do not climb alone; you climb together—you and your multidimensional selves. At this point in your life, the thrust of energy is designed to take you into the home of spirit where, with your accumulated knowledge, you will reflect upon your experiences and get a glimpse from the peak of your purpose for living. The vibration of faith, gained from passing through the dark territories, is your reward. Use it to take the dark energy, in need of love and healing, to the peak of the mountain with you. This act of internal balance is in essence a spiritual quest and connects you to the Gods as if they had sent a telegram saying, "You are called to our home now. Come and bring us the tales of your feats, for you have journeyed far in your reinterpretations of living. We would be glad to hear of what you know, and what you seek at this point of your initiation." You are, dear friends, in a global initiation of realization, and once you have been initiated, you will then go on to show the way, to teach about the new territory of thought you have pioneered; however, right now you are still climbing toward the peak one step at a time.

Your life is interconnected to the lives of many others, yet because you experience so little of the electromagnetic band of existence, you do not always understand the multiplicity of your dramas, which can appear to be isolated and connected only to you. Remember, educational systems have been based on isolation and separation: isolation from yourselves, and separation from others. Integrating and uniting with your mental, physical, spiritual, and emotional selves will connect you to the home of spirit; be aware that the players in your dramas also experience something similar. Third-dimensional experience offers a unique opportunity. You are connected to many other beings, and the lessons in living and the dramas they currently experience are parallel to yours to some degree; however what you experience in 3-D ripples outward in a unique way. You are a focal point in time because of Earth's destiny and what is occurring here. We sometimes call it the Big Cosmic Show, the fleeting moment of time between 1987 and 2012 where you move from the deepest of density to the highest of frequencies, and where you extend from third-dimensional living to span the electromagnetic band.

Another unique ability of yours is that you can manifest, in a very profound way, what others cannot. You are alive in an extremely dense aspect of existence, yet you are continuously flooded with the energy of the higher frequencies, which are based on instantaneous thought. Now, higher frequency does not imply something better; it is more like a reference point, similar to the way notes on a musical scale are used for describing the vibrations of sound frequencies and how they are expressed within a slice of time. The lower the frequency, the less rapid the vibration occurs within a parallel or similar slice of time. However, when you start to vibrate more rapidly in the third-dimensional world, you can span many realities and access great healing abilities from within.

In general, you do not live for a great expanse of time, usually at best ten decades; however your ancestors sometimes lived for thousands of years, as written in the old books. Your ancestors, no matter which way you trace them, were celestials; and, even more than that, no matter which way you trace them, you will discover that your ancestors were reptilian. In addition there are other numerous forms of intelligence who parade in and out of the laboratory offering their protocol and prospectus on how to treat and deal with humans. Remember, you can be adjusted and altered by vibrations because everything is vibration, and in 3-D your lives are currently challenged by the use of mind control through technologies that can influence every area of your lives. You must also take note that other beings, whom you cannot see, can affect you through frequency modulation from their dimension, tuning frequencies that adjust you on a cellular level. Comets, the sun, and the moon all hold frequencies that modulate you in a particular way, affecting the expression of your DNA in the cells of your body and the rate at which you grow in awareness.

The purpose of living is to grow, and the fear you meet on your path, whatever your fear happens to be, is your form of the dark. The collective global fear is that of being in charge of oneself, so you give others your power of decision-making, and in their need to live up to your expectations, they have chosen a dark dark practice of power. This is part of the hidden wound in need of healing that you carry to the mountain. In one way or another, you are seeing a family member, friend, or yourself challenged to heal the wound of the human spirit, a wound that ripples throughout time and deep within the human psyche, a wound truly about separation and isolation. Contemplate this thought for a moment: You have, in late-twentieth- and early-twenty-first-century Earth, become completely isolated from the majesty of spirit that is all around you; yet that hidden blanket of aliveness is now unfurling and there is no stopping it.

With this knowledge that we share, support yourself and your loved ones as you heal the wounds of the human psyche. Be encouraged to learn from their wounds as they mirror your own life—and that of others—and the purpose of living. If you use the knowledge as a reflection on living and where the season of change can take you, you will find the hidden message and meaning of the collective human wound. You will take this realization to the highest place you can; then finding the opportunity at the peaks of destiny, you will return to bring your insight and knowledge into the valleys where most humans dwell, encouraging them to climb the mountain themselves. And then the journey continues, for you are wayshowers for many realms of frequencies. The ability to transmute fear by finding the significant purpose of it on a personal, communal, global, and galactic level is another lesson you are here to learn.

The Gods, who jumped the electromagnetic spectrum and left footprints of an enigmatic nature in your world, are waiting for something from you and are not necessarily aware of it. Although you consider these beings as all-knowing and omniscient, you must realize they are not so different from you; yet they have their own unique perspective on existence. The home of the Gods is not necessarily a place where all knowingness and benevolence exist, and it is not as miraculous as you may think. Theirs is a different science, one you have yet to discover. Your science is based on demonstrability and repetition, on a conglomeration of theories that, if experientially replicated time and time again, become foundation principles. Many scientists on your world—Mendel for example with his genetic discoveries or Kepler with his astronomy and astrology studies—have pioneered new interpretations of reality. Today, scientists old and new will be awed and humbled by the massive reinterpretation of reality you are challenged to build. You will find that the closer you are to the end of the fleeting moment, your lessons about reality mirroring itself and that the part cannot be separated from the whole will drastically accelerate. Theory upon theory, premise upon premise, and foundation upon radical foundation will be flipped over and discarded, and new ideas will continuously appear, simultaneously transmitted so that all of you can catch them at once, as discoverers of the same point of light.

It is wise to question where this transmission originates. The Gods, as we said, laid down their supply lines and stored their stuff, a cache of materials they would need while under siege or when stranded in time. In many ways the Gods are trapped right now and do not know how to move beyond where they are. They experience an aspect of reality that is far more expansive than yours. They jump time lines and traverse existence with the flip of an internal frequency and can appear as humans—a leader of a country, a movie star, an athlete—from all walks of life. Yet they do not have the imprinting of a birth resulting from sexual union, the dynamic thrust of energy, the biological linkup of spiritual, emotional, physical, and mental bodies that creates your life. This fusion of two bodies, creating a frequency that welcomes in new life, allows you to experience a band of existence, a perspective or point of view that can never be attained without a sexual coupling.

We offer you a reflection of who you are, so you can create new probabilities in the Book of Earth, probabilities based on exalted learning where you transcend limited thinking, turning your lessons into gems of living. You were born to experience the spectrum of frequencies from the most dense to the highest, and the Gods knew this in their application of experience and ideal wisdom. The Gods live long, and sometimes they live with their lessons, their fear, their pain, and with the repetition of cycles much longer than you can imagine. You may appear to live with greater angst and emotional interaction with existence; however many of the beings you call Gods exist in a longevity of time that is immense. They have become prisoners in their own minds, prisoners of pain are these ancient beings. Various forms of intelligence will appear in greater numbers than ever, as the development of your psychic senses allows you to access paranormal experiences and otherworldly domains. The Gods or multidimensionals are connected to you, and not only do you broadcast to them, they also send messages back to you.

The fear you carry to the high peak has much more meaning than you assign to it. Whatever meanings you hold today are fine, and yet the meanings will grow and grow in time, backward and forward. You carry out a task for many dimensional beings other than yourselves, and they send you solutions through your fiduciaries that they themselves cannot execute because, in their versions of reality, change to the degree required now is not as easy for them as it is for you. You are the agents of change, and the ability to change and transmute your lives is yours again and again to marvel over, as you proclaim how well events unfold when you embrace faith and learn your lessons in living. There are no bad lessons, yet because you are afraid to know the dark and never study it, you turn what you fear and do not understand into the guise of darkness. Some of you never leave the swamplands because you do not have the courage, with the fear that you carry, to climb the mountain. And so transmute you must, for yourselves, for all of humankind, and most essentially, for your reptilian family whose wounds, like yours, go very very deep.

Everything is imbued with knowledge, and you are a part of a huge hologram, where one small fragment of anything contains the whole, and so you must learn to access the part, and then understand that the part cannot be separated from the whole. Over the next number of years, greater parts of the Story of Existence will appear as pieces of the puzzle. Pay close attention because as each step takes you farther up the mountain, each new discovery will be a thread brought forth from Earth and the heavens, from memories on the corridors of time, weaving significant tales about the majesty of your lineage. The Gods stashed their greatest victory and aspiration in you, knowing that when reality shut down and the potential gridlock occurred, you had been given the keys to unlock realities everywhere. These are lofty concepts, yet this is the quest you are on, which takes place from moment to moment in the privacy and significance of your life. So breathe deep and look around, knowing you are called upon to expand your worldview, to sit in the home of spirit and share what you know; to hear and see and to experience what the world is like from the peaks of existence.

Those of you who are mountain climbers know that, when you are at the top of a mountain, the energies are rarefied and often great clarity comes to those who climb. Mountain climbers sometimes carry burdens or problems on their backs, and when they get to the top of the mountain, they have the solutions. Mountains serve as huge antennas reaching up into the atmosphere—remember your atmosphere is imprinted with life—and so you climb the mountains to breathe the most rarefied of air, clear your head, and reach the peak where all existence can be seen.

Can all humans be traced to one ancestor? Is there such a being? Legends on Earth seem to imply as much, although there were certainly primary Gods, secondary Gods, and tertiary Gods. In ancient times the ancestors knew that these Gods battled in the heavens and appeared periodically in their ships of light, causing shakings and thundering of the Earth. They were sometimes afraid of the Gods, and sometimes they prepared for their coming. Huge underground structures were built long ago—tunnels and cities in South America, Asia Minor, and China. All over your globe are yet-to-be-discovered underground dwellings that housed many many people—even whole civilizations. This gives you something to ponder. Why would your ancestors build cities underground? What beings periodically visited the planet, leaving their tracks and trails in every legend and mythology, using myriad names and cavorting in different capacities? The legends appear to be similar from continent to continent. These visitors literally exist in another dimension and periodically intercede in yours, and when they are invisible, it simply means that you do not see them, yet they still can influence you.

As you climb, you will see other peaks, and you will view the home of spirit and the Gods, eventually realizing that the Gods and their families are vast. In your desire for a single

God, you have confused your God with the singularity of the force of love, the unified field that connects you and everything else to experienced existence. You are all part of a presence, a hologram of omniscient knowing, the field of love that is in every frequency spectrum, in every universe. In essence, the field of love is the ultimate source, and differentiates itself in every way possible. In your quest for a single deity, you have interpreted, to the best of your ability, the phenomena of UFOs and the intercession of the spirit world. Actually, forces from everywhere send you energies, and although sometimes they trick you, they also help you climb the mountain to view the greater vista of existence. How you respond is part of your living and the lessons you learn from one time to another. An immense mountain, a singular peak rising from the swamps, awaits you. From the top of this mountain, the highest some of you will ever climb, you will see a vast expanse of mountain peaks and may then realize there is no one mountain or one God. You do not have to climb every peak out there, yet by climbing a peak you can begin to see more, reconsidering what else is out there. When you reconsider your beliefs, your knowledge of and purpose in living expand.

Reflect on your life and recall your mystical experiences, and please do not hide these experiences because you are afraid to be labeled crazy or insane. You are now challenged to bring the mysterious, mystical home of spirit back to your planet because this is what is missing. The Gods await your announcements. They know you hold solutions, and that the frequency of love that you can create is the ultimate healing source. Like no other species in existence, you have been gifted with this capacity that has always been there as a potential. Many of you seek to increase your potential, which includes both mental and physical stamina, yet above all we ask you to seek out your potential to produce love. This is the gift stored within you that the Gods await. How you bring that love forward is of course up to you, since there are as many ways and varieties as there are plants and flowers, birds and bees upon your planet—as many varieties as the six billion Gods dare to decree.

It is important to understand that the act of transmutation you are called upon to experience is an act of divine love, intended to heal the dimensions of time. Time-jumpers and your ancestors will send you bits of knowledge because your Now is woven into theirs; however you are the head weaver, the one who is to decide which thread goes where, who checks the design to make certain that the pattern stays balanced. Your ancestors often left their keys of knowledge in patterns of fabrics and in weavings of rugs. You see the designs as beautiful pieces of art, yet if you were to study them and discover the truth, you would find they contain hidden codes and meanings, ciphers passed down through time for generations. Visit a museum or a place where artifacts are gathered; look at them and imagine their function being reinterpreted. Perhaps the masks and statues, tools and utensils, dolls, weapons, and everything you see are now coming alive, activated and ready to tell you a very different story than one that speaks predominantly of people divided and conquered. We ask you to look in every nook and cranny and open your mind to the idea that a completely different story waits to be interpreted by you.

As Pleiadian time-travelers, when we enter your world seeking to discover more of who we are, we do so knowing that reality exists as a mirror, and that the part cannot be separated from the whole. If this is true, and we continue to find it so, then it seems to us that, if the part cannot be separated from the whole and reality mirrors itself, eventually everything becomes united and reaches a stage of complete self-knowing. Your theories about the formation of existence include the movements of expansion and contraction. You continuously experience these movements from moment to moment in your life as you breathe: You breathe in the vital force, fill your lungs and then empty them. Even though most of you breathe unconsciously, the message is still intact: expand and contract, expand and contract, since you need both actions to live and experience the fullness of existence. Your job as Family of Light is to weave all the pieces together, to consider all actions, and when you experience an uncomfortable area, realize it is time to reassess your beliefs and assumptions about reality, to see them in a completely new light.

A change of administration is always accompanied by a bit of scuffling, and your Gods have certainly left such tales in your history books. Massive galactic battles have transpired, and Earth has been to some a sanctuary, a place where they have fled from the great battles. Science fiction novels and movies about space travel—stories of light and dark—are part of the cellular memory that you are learning to understand and address. You will eventually discover an influence that is vast, so vast it will seem impossible for your mortal third-dimensional mind to fathom, just as a mere five decades ago numbers in the trillions were difficult for you to imagine. You will eventually become accustomed to and feel at home with the vastness of the spiritual domain; it is comparable to starting off with simple computer programs, then signing on to the Internet where there is so much more from which to choose. The times propel you to create new neurological patterns in your being, and what seems at first to be too much stimulation, eventually becomes manageable. Every species goes through a similar process of an expansion of consciousness when it is their time.

The Gods fought their battles over who would be in charge, and at one time every culture had stories of the mother and father Gods and their children. Sometimes their children mated with humans, creating the demi-Gods and extending their hierarchies farther away from the mother/father Gods' influence. Often your ancestors built pyramids to

delineate the levels or families of existence under whose influence they were subjected. Pyramids around the globe were
decorated with symbols of serpents, stars, moons, suns, and
disks, all of which hold significant keys to your understanding of the vast intelligences who, at different times, have influenced you. And we remind you once again that just
because you cannot see them and they do not appear to you,
does not mean they are not here. The Gods, in their own dimension, can affect you through the spectrum, an idea which
you need to grasp.

The standards of your living are an essential part of the
frequency you broadcast to all those connected to you. And
we say once again that it is essential for you to influence your
multidimensional selves by putting your frequency in the
ethers; your ancestors are relying upon you to do this because
their wounds are ancient and they do not know how to completely heal them. We have already suggested that the frequency of love is the common frequency of which everything
is composed, and that humans produce love in such a unique
way. In the making of a very fine wine, special grapes are
grown on select land, and in a specific cyclical season where
all conditions are ideal, these grapes for making the most exquisite wine are harvested. You are like the grapes in their season on a sequestered hillside, prepared in this season of
change to produce the most exquisite of elixirs and essences.
Your version of love at its finest is awaited, and even though
it may seem to be a small crop, a minor vintage so to speak,
when you produce your finest and allow it to spread, in the
bigger Book of Existence, it ripples outward beyond your
Now, affecting the whole. Everything is frequency, and it only
takes a little shift in frequency to affect all other frequencies.
So as frequency beings, you are to become aware, to transmute and expand, and to enter into the home of spirit as people who lead people to lead themselves.

Because the Gods influence you, the energies of their unresolved family dramas are transferred as frequency to your world. You may say, "Are family fights not natural?" Yes, it is true, there are disagreements and arguments within families; however violence is unnecessary. Violence is the opposite of love and creates a divide-and-conquer syndrome through separation and isolation. The wounds of the Gods—wounds of separation, of fear and terror, of being alone and not knowing how to deal with it—are no greater than your own; they just exist longer and affect more people, more of existence. In their own arrogance, the Gods have been so immersed in their power that they are unable to step back and reflect on what they create. Empathy, the ability to feel for others, is unknown to these Gods, and for you it is one of your greatest characteristics. Raising your frequency and producing your version of the vibration of love is based upon your ability to feel deep pain, fear, anxiety, discordance, confusion, and chaos; to go into those feelings, survive them, and to find peace once again. Use your will to create peace within yourself and your life, and resolve that all situations shall turn into opportunities. Many beings await your courage to carry on with these momentous tasks, which you think you carry alone as your own private fears, when in actuality your fears are manifestations of the great separation and wounds of the Gods, your ancestors throughout time.

Now knowing all of this and that the Book of Earth is connected to all of existence, perhaps you will walk lighter as you climb, straightening your shoulders and breathing deeper into your body than you ever have and saying, "Ah, is that what's going on? Now that I know of the quest for myself and a reinterpretation for all humanity, then of course I shall do it." Remember that you have free will in each moment to create a unique and brand new version of existence, yet those moments are also overlaid in time and can be looked at backward and forward as if they were solid events having already occurred.

Your free will can only be exercised by you. Of course destinies exist, yet some destinies are ignored and never chosen, and every moment holds the potential for you to think of a new option, to receive a unique idea in the fleeting moment of time. Using your will, entwined with knowing that you live a significant life, allows you to translate your experience into wisdom. The Gods believe that they have held the truth for eons, as do the World Management Team and the Family of Dark. Actually, all people feel they hold truths, but today new truths are at hand, new philosophies and beliefs, completely unlike anything you have previously conceived. We do our best to name and describe what is occurring, yet in truth it is unnameable. We can barely scratch the surface with our descriptions of where you are headed, and like your ancestors, we have no words to describe the realms that await you; yet our words deliver a resonance and hidden meaning, a plan within a plan. No matter where you find yourself, know that one of the greatest truths of all is that everything is connected. Give up your sense of isolation, discovering that the part cannot be separated from the whole, for by knowing this you become part of the whole plan, and you will see plans within plans, within plans. No force of existence can ever implement its plan without other options existing from which to choose. In order to transmute a plan and participate from a higher place of awareness, you must remember and know where your power lies.

Imagine the entire world being reinterpreted to reveal people finding significance in the land they live on, feeling pride in the continent of their birth, looking across the mountains, swamps, valleys, and meadows, watching winds blow across deserts or howling through the tops of trees, hearing rain and thunder, and seeing the wonder of polar lights and full and dark moons. Imagine people everywhere feeling the call to understand the highest knowledge, to view living from the peaks.

Legends in the Cosmos

Five hundred years ago your European ancestors were confronted with the fact that the Earth was round, not a flat surface they were in peril of falling off; they had to grasp that they were living in a far more expansive realm than they had ever imagined. Even though ancient maps of Earth have always existed, with some showing Antarctica without the ice cap and islands in the northern regions, no one knew for certain what was out there because the real knowledge had been lost. Ignorance prevailed as separation became the mode of influence on your world: Separate the people, give them a divinity, and tell them their divinity is the only one. Today humankind has over two hundred thousand divinities, or religions that are all separated; yet during the bridging of an age, there is always an opportunity for unity.

From our experience we contend that wherever consciousness finds itself, it must locate and immerse itself there. You each have a name and address and use numbers for identification, yet some of you are afraid that through computer systems these names and numbers can be used to identify and locate you anywhere at any time. From our perspective, you are so much more than letters and numbers; you are energy. You are all Family of Light, whether you are a cousin's cousin one branch removed, or one of the staunchest of patriarchs and matriarchs, it makes no difference for you are destined to know what we share with you. As we see it in the Book of Earth, the test is to understand that you are all part of a genetic experiment, and as energies are received by you, you each choose them in very different ways. Yet, we see the bridge that you build, a bridge from everywhere and nowhere, that allows time-jumpers to enter and influence the outcome of this great era of creativity, where reality will be imprinted and set into motion for a period of time.

The influence of the stars and the heavens is important for you to recognize. On Earth you are enchanted and entertained with a moon that modulates and influences you. You will learn to communicate with this satellite to a greater degree when you understand that the moon has a story to tell, a story that holds many of the missing keys to the unfoldment of your consciousness. The vast heavens are filled with a movement that has been recorded in calendars of stone from around the planet, pointing out solstice and equinox positions, as well as noting various star systems. These indicators are by design and not by accident. Your ancestors understood cosmic principles that you laugh at today thinking them unimportant, yet they were able to live with their cosmic cousins, the stellar beings, the celestial visitors who came from the stars and through the dimensions. As the great fan of existence unfolds into this time of immense power, consider what you will do with that power. Do you dream of being a time-jumper, caught up in the tangled corridors of time, seeding yourself everywhere and thinking that no one will ever suspect it? The Gods themselves have these abilities, and yet everything is connected and nothing happens without consequences: Little parts of them get separated everywhere throughout time, billions and trillions and quadrillions of years, beyond what you can conceive. And even though the separation is immense, it is still part of a vast intelligence that monitors itself and stays connected to all parts of itself because that is its power.

The energy that comes to you, as we have said, is designed and planned. As a genetic experiment, you are a small fraction of the vastness of existence, a speck; however, as we have also said, from our point of view you are a priceless speck, a unique jewel, majestically and magically magnificent. Now, the quest for answers always leads to greater questions as you are discovering, and yet it is this questing that truly imbues you, and certainly us, with the spark of life. When you lose interest in the place where you find yourself, then the game is over! Many of you wonder what you will do in a world activated by this energy. How will you live? Where will you live? What will you do? Your real work is to expand your consciousness, allowing this energy of change to move through you, and when it changes your old ways of thinking, then the patterns of your life will stop repeating themselves and you will be open to new possibilities. In the past few days, weeks, months, how many repetitive patterns have you experienced? If your dramas are repeating themselves, step back, take a look, and realize that this area of your life needs change. Changing involves giving up specific thoughts, feelings, actions, and behaviors, seeing them as beliefs about reality. You are often glued shut like the little seed with a hard casing; although, if you remember, when the casing cracks the seed lets go of what it no longer needs. When this occurs, life for the seed becomes smoother, and so you too are called forth, like the seed, to sprout upward and reach into the rays of the sun and the rays of cosmic change.

It is important to realize that those who encourage you to be in fear of change influence the kind of energies you put out. When you are in fear, the vibration you transmit has a jagged edge to it. When you exude an energy of confidence, faith, and love, and are open to receive power, while being humble at the same time, your field is strong and expansive. A humble recognition of the power of power, as well as clear codes of conduct, is an essential map of understanding that will help you assess what may lie ahead and give you courage to face the future. We look at the Book of Earth and see probabilities, and we will say this: There is a point to the nanosecond of time, the twenty-five-year period you are so privileged to live; it is to transmute yourself from dense beings to the highest of frequencies. You are envied and watched, but these energies do not come to destroy you; they are here to amplify and bring out the best in your genetic line. Many people do not understand what is occurring, and they may think it unfair to be subjected to a plan, and to whose plan? We are always mentioning the Gods, your ancestors, and we do so quite ambiguously to avoid overdefining them so as to allow your time lines, your DNA, and the window between your eyebrows—the place that you have learned to energize—to show you where you have come from, where you are going, and the cosmic plans that involve you.

Within the nanosecond, the closer one gets to the year 2000, the more difficult it appears to be to access Earth, for it seems that certain frequencies have, let us say, set up roadblocks, and that is fine. It tells us that you will have to deal with what you have created. Yet, for those of you who have a connection to the vistas of higher consciousness, where you feel your link to the spiritual world as a rightful inheritance and live it peacefully in the most ordinary way, these lines will never be closed down. They are rich with life and exquisitely encoded to be open for you; however you must seek them out. And the closer the nanosecond is to completion by the end of 2012, the more difficult it is for time-jumpers to come in, as well as for viewers of this section of the Book of Earth to see exactly what transpires. It appears that there is a void, as if certain portions of the Book have been blacked out, censored perhaps, or cordoned off. Roadblocks for protection, or defense? It is all the same. It makes little difference whether the plan is one of light or one of dark, since each family is part of the whole, which you must remember as power becomes yours.

In days long past on your planet, there were many stories and tales of dragons and magicians, of beings who flew in the heavens, as well as humans who invoked the heavens and were taken up into the sky. These tales have peppered your legends, yet in most cases, the moderns of today believe these stories are figments of ancestral imagination. By visiting museums, you allow yourself to reconsider the information there, so be open to the impulses of knowledge that will come through you. As the energies flow into and around the Earth, be in wonder like children first learning about the world. Wonder about the unfoldment of knowledge, rather than knowing about it. There is an old saying in the Book of Earth, and it appears again and again: "The more you learn the less you know." And that saying is found in other books that tell about existence in other places where you find yourselves with other names, other corporeal realities, and a different consciousness.

Remember, the fiduciary's job is to keep the books and manage them for you, as well as to keep you informed in an honest way as to what connects you to the business of living. Nonetheless, you are sometimes overwhelmed: You bounce checks, forget to take the garbage out on the right day; you are recycling, paying bills, doing the laundry and dry-cleaning, shopping for groceries, and picking up the kids. These activities occupy your living, but you are coming now to a time of change where you will no longer do many of them. Do not mourn the past. Some of you live for the good old days, yet the good old days are being made in the present. The Now, the place where you find yourself, is where we want you to be ripe, full, and alive because you are presently the seedling, the kernel, and the sprout of what you will become.

Much of existence is focused on you at this time, although that is not to say everyone has their telescopes pointed at Earth. However, there are legends in the cosmos, just as there are legends on Earth, and cosmic legends speak of this time of change and refer to you as a gem of a genetic library tucked away, an experiment made for a "just-in-case" time. And this experiment has been fought over and discounted, recognized and forgotten, valued and given away; you have experienced all these events in the collective of your consciousness, in the cells of who you are. Five hundred years ago your ancestors were not called upon to have their cells awaken in the way your cells are. In the annals of time, in the Book of Earth, these opportunities to awaken do not appear that often.

As we have said, the cycle you find yourself in is the 26,000-year precession of the equinoxes, divided into twelve eras, with the imprint of twelve having a profound effect on your system—clocks, calendars, and configurations of twelve are found everywhere. You carry an imprint that organizes your world around the numeral twelve; it is part of your time cycle so to speak, affecting the core of your being. It appears to us that as the nanosecond closes, and you reach 2012, you will move to the next counting of time. Time is arbitrary and never definitive; however everything is significant and connected in time, even randomly occurring phenomena like the placement of the moon in perfect configuration with the sun, so that they appear to be of the same size.

And even though there are plans within plans, do not think Family of Dark has the final plan, nor does Family of Light. You may wonder who has the final plan, and who or what is the Maker. The Maker is the great force you are required by destiny and self-decree to produce for existence, for yourselves, and for the experiment. You are the Gods' secret tucked away in time, and they wait to see if you can change from one form of being into another in a nanosecond—in their terms; in yours, perhaps it takes a lifetime, a lifetime enriched and extraordinary, above and beyond ordinary existence. You have an exquisite opportunity to create a completely unique kind of power and to bring purposefulness and meaning to Earth. Cosmic legends are full of this tale about you humans. Just as your legends on Earth are filled with tales of magicians, at this juncture in time you are looked upon in the Book of Earth as magicians yourselves, the whole lot of you, not simply a few. The heavens hold the rich imprint of electromagnetic aliveness, and as you move through space, your planet, solar system, and galaxy all traverse new territory. This territory has been planned for you to encounter, one that will recode your DNA in this lifetime to connect you to the multidimensional intelligence that exists beyond your biology, and is your inheritance.

We have said that the Book of Earth was made by ordinary men and women, most of whose names never appear in your history books, people who never led battles or coups, yet the richness of their existence, their knowledge, and their abilities were imprinted in the blood they passed along to you. Remember, your ancestral lineage is rich, and is there for you to pick and choose from, to decide which aspects of power and creativity you wish to cultivate. Rulebreakers are often the ones who explore new territory, and some rules are made to be broken, especially the rules that inhibit your freedom and tell you what to think, instead of encouraging you to become a creative, thinking, and perceiving part of a loving whole. The ruler of the plan, above and beyond the plans of Family of Light and Family of Dark, is the force called love.

All of this may appear to be an enigma, a paradox to baffle your being. You are legends in the making and have already created the legends, because as we have said, periods of time can be approached from any direction, although every once in a while a fragment of time can appear to be quarantined. In that case, warning signs are posted saying that the time site is overloaded with too many visitors, like on your Internet. Computer linkups can serve as a model of sorts for time-jumping, although of course time-jumping is much more fantastic. As you expand your consciousness, you build constructs outside of yourself to mirror the greater workings of existence. Your creativity works this way, yet so often you create without wit or wisdom. You become so enamored of inventions that you miss their purpose, which is to present you with a model of the universe. Again we mention that you are biological beings of impeccable design. If you grasp this truth, then you will build a bridge of great strength and will weave around the darkness, leaving it to discover itself and to eventually realize that to create destruction is to set the course for self-destruction. Through the cosmic calendar and the timing of events, this truth is coming home to roost, so to speak.

The moon makes thirteen cycles, from new to full, in one of your years, yet your modern calendar focuses on a solar year of twelve months. Contemplating the number thirteen as a hidden mystery will bring an understanding of what influences you. Although thirteen has been considered a number of ill luck and evil, if you search you will find that it holds a very powerful key for decoding the consciousness of humankind. The years in the declining portion of the nanosecond leading to 2012 will fly by like months to you. Those who exist in a much larger expanse of time must fine-tune their focus to capture this fleeting twenty-five-year nanosecond. No easy task. If you wonder what this may be like, find a nanosecond in your own life and then see if you can continuously enter it and find the richness it holds, comparing it to twenty-five years of your time. It seems impossible to do; how could it be? Perhaps you cannot yet imagine that a technology could be designed where someone would say, "Look, let's take a second that already happened, locate a nanosecond of it, and then extend it into twenty-five years so we can see what's there." Based on your science, you would see emptiness, that nothing would be there. How could something so little contain anything? Yet if you think about it, your place within the heavens is a mere speck of littleness as well. How could you be? How could your life be so full and complex and burdensome and joyful? How could it be so rich and alive? And yet in the vastness of everything, in the Book of Existence, how much space would you take up?

The builders of the bridge of light will accomplish much, although they have many challenges to face in the years ahead. Remember, it will never pay to attack, condemn, or destroy another. It is truly to your benefit as Family of Light to take on this awesome task and be gracious, intent upon finding solutions. You are not to ignore challenges or difficulties, and in looking at the purpose of the dark, you will see a need to heal. A time will come when you will be called upon to be great visionaries, to imagine an outcome that may seem impossible and to trust yourselves with a faith that seems beyond what you ever could imagine. All over the world on every continent chaos will reign. Chaos can arouse fear; however fear is a choice. In times past, in times simultaneous, and even in times of the future, there are always those who choose fear, yet not all of your ancestors did. Victors write the books of fear where the victims are conquered, although to be conquered, you must first believe you are a victim. This is the choice you too shall make: victims or creators? Remember, victims choose fear and become paralyzed, and the vibration sent out is quite jagged and discordant.

Chaos is part of the time of change; it is a dismantling process and a time of confusion, where one is not certain of anything, except for a certain aliveness that accompanies its arrival. It appears in the Book of Earth that the more secure you feel, the more complacent you become, and then the easier it is for others to influence, manage, and control your thinking process. Confusion can serve many purposes; for it can ultimately introduce a new order. Leadership everywhere attempts to create order, to hold power for you, because you do not want it yourselves. So we ask you always to question whose order is being introduced. Remember there are plans within plans, and no matter whose order is the plan of the day, those of you who are wise and aware know there is always another plan, another order, an order so mysterious one must initiate oneself to a new way of perceiving and thinking to read it. We do our best to describe this order in words so you can capture words in books, study them and nod your heads and say, "Yes, I am aware of this force."

In your desire to experience tactile living, you have become so busy with constructing and building that you have forgotten about connections. Throughout the last few ages, it appears that your ancestors did not have as many material objects and as much busyness to occupy themselves. They did not have the elaborate highway systems for traveling, or the electronics, commerce, sports, and entertainment that you do. Living was different for them, and yet they were very alive. The season of change that you find yourself within asks you to be more alive as well. Chaos has its own order and creates an aliveness that balances and finely tunes the senses, making you more keenly aware of the food you eat, especially if you are short of funds, or if the shelves in the store are empty and the food in the garden is not yet ready. Chaos shall bring a new order, an order that has to do with spiritual organization, one with no speaker or head of the pyramid.

Ancient legends are filled with tales of those who evoked higher powers, of extraordinary magicians who appeared one moment and were gone the next, and of your legendary ancestors the dragons who both provoked and protected humankind. These stories are not mere flights of fancy, figments of imagination, or whims of a delightful pen. The ethers are alive, and the electromagnetic spectrum is a storehouse of frequencies through which you can surf existence. Your physical bodies are designed to respond to the encoding in the coming energy, which you would consider a miracle if you knew it was happening. A miracle, dear friends, that you can muck up because nothing is guaranteed! There is always the choice of freedom, even within the tyrannies, and freedom is so vast that it allows the tyrannies their reigns.

In the later years of this fleeting moment in time, you will see radical changes everywhere. Structures of authority will crumble, and the great halls of congresses and parliaments, places where the voices of authority spoke, will be empty. This is not something we see as ominous or fearful; it is something that happens, and a groundswell of relief will arise within people, and a renaissance will appear to be at hand, one based on a psychic connection and the need for one another, not on outside authority. We see this realization in certain fragments of the Book of Earth; however we cannot see everything. As we have said, some vistas are cordoned off so there will be no interference and you can deal with what you have created. And if it is tyranny you create, then you will find yourselves in a dark corridor of time. The cordoned-off area allows you to move forward uninterrupted—into dark or light—whatever you choose, for at some point you must manifest. So the chaos ultimately brings you the opportunity to connect and manifest, and eventually you will discover what it is to be a community, although for now you must each see if you are qualified to lead yourself. We know you are ready and qualified. The question is, do you?

We can look at the Book of Earth backward, forward, and sideways in time, and we see the impulses and the plans, the designing of family lines, the genetic matings, and the passing of certain traits through to all of you, not just a few. The ruling families on your planet know the significance of the number thirteen and steer you away from its use, convincing you that it is the number of ill luck or evil. However, it is a key to the doorway of the mystery of power, and remember that you cannot avoid power. As humankind, more power is coming to you, and this is decreed in the books and by the force itself. Before you can build a true community where you live connected with each other and with dimensional and celestial beings as well, you must first feel qualified to lead yourself. Are you autonomous and in charge? Are you comfortable being the creator, the designer of your own reality? This is being asked of you, and once it is asked, you cannot turn your back on power. Do your best. Hold your chin high and your spine straight, breathe into your lungs the fullness that you are and see yourself as an energetic being, vibrating the energies you choose through your will and intent. No matter what probabilities and choices are presented, always know that spirit is around you and speaks through you, to you, with you, and for you—and even against you, as a test.

You must be alert and gather your wits, and ideally our tales remind you to do this. Remember the magicians of old held their secrets, as did the dragons in their legends. The dragons had many wonderful gifts, and enlivened numerous civilizations on your world. Now you are wondering, are they the creatures depicted in books, calendars, and cards? Are they real? You are living in a time when the word real, just as the word truth, will be redefined, expanded upon, and understood in a different light. Many of your legends and myths are very real. At the closing of the nanosecond, the creatures in these myths and legends will all return; you will see them first in your imagination, as the cells in your body release their story when the Earth vibrates at a new frequency and breathes a sigh of release through her magnetic field. You will find new data sprouting around you, and from geysers of knowledge inside yourselves information will spring forth, and you will need each other to weave it together and connect it to the whole. Remember you are always being given threads; a piece of thread is fine in itself, but woven together the threads create an even finer tapestry.

The implosion of knowledge leads you to your power as

living biological beings, and this is happening to everyone everywhere: people on the streets, those sequestered away in nursing homes, hospitals, and prisons; it happens on the playgrounds, in schools, the workplace, out on the pastoral lands, in the fields, on the mountaintops, and in the valleys. In every land where the sun rises and sets, Family of Light and Family of Dark live. And who are those in between, who claim kin to neither and who would think this tale a rambling, ranting rave? Who are they? We ask you to ask yourself; you are after all, all humankind. Rather than claim overallegiance to either light or dark, ground yourself and explore what you all have in common: your humanness, for it is this quality that so many have sought.

The legends of dragons are rich, and richer still are stories of the legendary lizards. The ancient manuscripts and books that have been sequestered away, particularly in religious centers, place their kind everywhere. Around the globe in all of the halls of knowledge, invented and true, you will find Family of Light willing to remember, willing to weave the story of unity and wholeness, of power and purposeful living. The ancient lizards and dragons were very fascinated with humans; as the story goes they are responsible for your creation, or so they feel and believe. They have mated with you, studied you, taught you, cherished you, and helped you establish civilization, and they have also raised you to devour and consume you. As third-dimensional beings, you see yourselves in one way; however the legendary lizards, ancestors of all the ancient ones—the elders of long ago—see you in a different way. You are part human to them, yet they see you across the spectrum of existence, and know the strength of your humanity. They count on your predictability, and yet they also know that, in the Book of Earth at this time, a wild card is being dealt.

Everything you have learned is being tested now, and the cream of the crop will produce the most exquisite of elixirs, the elixir of the love frequency. One of your tests today is understanding frequency: your ability to recognize it, to know that you have always been producing it, and will continue to produce frequency whether you are dead or alive. Your challenge is to modulate frequency to change your mode of living from the repetition of dramas that usually zap your health and take your spirit away. You must learn to recognize what does not work for you, then release your fears and change; this action will modify the frequency and vibration that you broadcast. This lesson, dear friends, is being taught to you in kindergarten, the essence of this phase of your education. Before you can read the Book of Existence, you must understand the Book of Earth.

Remember, as the century closes a new one begins, and even though your marking of time is an arbitrary, convenient, local custom, it is also part of a larger marking of the divine plan. Everything is coded: the cells of your body, your DNA, the air you breathe, the living biological library, the ether, and the heavens. No matter what you think you invent or conjure and bring into form, we remind you that it is never an isolated event; everything is always connected to something else. Plans within plans within plans will reveal themselves; so we ask you, dear friends, to rest assured that as Family of Light, wanting a peek at the Book of Earth to see what lies ahead, there is something exquisite that you can create. What it is, we do not know. We will do our best to inspire you to create a new vision of your future; however you must first make a self-assessment. What do you want to build in this time of immense change? If your ancestors truly are living legends returning as dragons, reptiles, and multidimensional creatures, and as your biological human ancestors speak to you, and as all of this power comes to you, the sense of connectedness, of knowing that past mysteries had meaning—stones, crosses, crystals, chalices of blood, caches of gold, steeds of great power, and beasts that surface from the deepest oceans—if all of this is real, what world will you build? The flatworlders did not think of these potentials when they set out five hundred years ago. They forgot they would become their own ancestors, and so they were easily steered to destruction, separation, and disconnected meaninglessness, and to competition and striving for material achievement. You have equated power with material consumption, collection, and hoarding. You admire people who have vast mansions, caches of gold, jewels, and trinkets to dazzle and befuddle the public. Is this really wealth and power? The real power lies in knowing the meaning of the song the birds sing, to be synchronized and harmonized by the sounds of Nature: the tree frogs, the insects, the whippoorwills, the calls of the mourning dove and the mockingbird, or the nightingale with its sweet sound at dusk.

Your lizard and dragon ancestors were multifaceted in their abilities to live because they understood the many aspects of civilization, of which creativity is one of the most powerful. For without creativity, individuality and life itself wither and fade away. This is part of the problem humankind faces today. An overfocus on the accumulation of material goods has allowed you to produce without creativity and meaning, to engineer a sameness, a replication, to keep all of you moving along the same path. In the ensuing years of chaos, great creativity will arise connected to a feminine principle intertwined with a strong, masculine principle, establishing a balance. At this stage you will begin to understand that the management of energy is your true quest for power. You cannot escape the fact that energy requires you to know it in the same way that the meaningful plan of spirit requires you to make it known in your home.

Do not be frightened of these times of change. If the words and concepts seem foreign to some of you, then remember your ancestors of five hundred years ago, when a whole new world was opening for them as well. For hundreds of years afterward, they traveled in ships on the oceans, still wondering if the great beasts of legends would arise and devour them. Some of the voyagers saw the movement of objects from the future in and out of the waters at night, but these mysteries were kept very quiet; if they spoke of such things, the label of insanity was quickly laid on them. The last five hundred years were times of great expansion; however there was also an immense control over how you would perceive this expansion. In reflecting upon your ancestors throughout time, we ask you to open up to your genetic inheritance and to consider without judgment the challenges your ancestors faced. From the top of the mountain that you have climbed, know that you are at the pinnacle of comprehension for now, so what conclusions do you draw? What is the total of your knowledge? Do your wisdom and living flourish?

The dragons of renown are nameless creatures, but they are not formless; they have many personalities and are shape-shifters who embody a magnificent force. You have a similar force in your body; however it is disavowed, beaten, or enslaved, rarely encouraged to develop. Your traditions call this force the fire of life, the flame of existence, and the kundalini or the inner serpent that rises within you. All traditions speak of and weave their meanings and symbolic interpretations around the legends of your ancestors, the great reptiles and dragons. Now, imagine that these creatures live around you and they have not been visible to your eye because they live in other dimensions and domains. The electromagnetic spectrum, the band of existence, houses them right next to your address, yet you cannot see them. Earlier we suggested taking any nanosecond, a billionth of a second as you count time, and breaking it down to find twenty-five years' worth of living. You may think the place is empty, yet in actuality it is where the dragons dwell, where the ancient reptilian lineage that is your inheritance calls home.

So, will you build a technology that breaks down time to

examine your own seconds and discover new frontiers and territories within nanoseconds? If you accomplish this feat, have compassion for what you experience. In addition, vistas of reality may appear to you, and you will think them distinctly alive and real, as if you turned a dial to find yourself poised in another world, and yet you will know without a doubt that you are located in late-twentieth-century- or early-twenty-first-century Earth. This experience will become commonplace and may create many casualties; some people will be very frightened for their sanity, even if they have joyous experiences. You must encourage the exploration within and create a vibration of safety. An exquisite opportunity exists through the services of the fiduciary to enliven and uplift your spirit.

You strive for this fulfillment when you decode the number thirteen, and see the 26,000-year precession cycle divided by thirteen rather than twelve. The missing thirteenth slice was always there, just like the thirteen moons. We ask you to consider that the numbers twelve and thirteen mean much more than you have understood, and we will assure you of that. Through language and numbers, everything is coded—backward, forward. As you learn to read energy, you will recognize it as your inheritance of power; and as you become managers of energy, you will see the aliveness and purposefulness of existence and that deception cannot hold truth. And what, you may ask, is truth? Truth is where no secrets are kept, that is truth.

A healing occurs in the sharing of knowledge and in the revealing of secrets. Secrets are very hard to keep; they weigh a lot, and are heavy and burdensome. Secrets are often the beginning of lies; one lie breeds another, and liars attract liars, and this is the nature of lies. On your world, power has not been shared as energy; it has been held in secrecy and based on lies. We ask you to consider that those in positions of power are really magicians of energy, whether they are self-willed and self-proclaimed or in total ignorance. Leaders are jugglers of energy and knowing this, we ask each of you now to juggle your own energy, to know that energy is free and around you waiting for you to direct it. You are the conductor of a magnificent symphony of creation that will outperform everything that has ever been staged.

The ancient ones, the dragons, wait; they want to be discovered, to return to Earth and reveal what they know without harming you, but you must create the frequency within yourselves to see them and to assist them to heal whatever schisms they have in their own family line. It is not only you who must heal yourselves; all of existence is looking to be reconnected. What is healing, and how do you know when you are healed? A flow of energy accompanies a healing, like a goose with a golden egg! This flow of energy fills you with the confidence and faith to move forward; it is a connection to what you call spirit, a connection to all of existence. And healing, as we have mentioned, is reinterpreting what you believe happened to you. Your wounds start because of how you feel and because you hold such strong feelings; you have become afraid of your feelings, and your feelings are where you keep yourselves as prisoners. Suppressed feelings build and accumulate like a ball of yarn; they can block the flow of energy in your being, and sometimes the ball needs to be unraveled and rewoven into a meaningful pattern rather than blocking the flow. Energy is energy. It responds to your intent and to electrical impulses. Your power will grow rapidly as Earth gives her magnetic sigh, as the magnetic field lessens its grip and the elements in your periodic table begin to jiggle and dance and molecules begin to speed up, opening new paradigms of experience to be discovered.

Now that you have scaled the peaks, you know you must manage energy in order to design your future. We see various probable futures, and time-jumpers are very aware that, at this point in time, a number of probabilities spring from Earth, many based on great manipulation and control. However, in those darkened-out areas and corridors where time-jumpers cannot enter, only you who live there can use your golden opportunity to build the bridge, building it perhaps beyond the mere span of an age. From the peak you can see that you have much more to consider. Take it easy on this journey, knowing you will always learn more, and that the more you learn, the more there is to learn. Be humble and give thanks as the force of existence responds to your gratitude.

The Gods Stashed their Stuff

In the Book of Earth, the section of existence where you currently find yourself in the weavings of the lines of time is in need of a vision based on a collective purpose for humankind, a vision where significant living is recognized and pursued. This task may seem overwhelming if your focus is totally immersed in linear time in the third dimension. However time, as we have suggested, can be approached backward, forward, and sideways, from within and without, and is all based on energy and frequency; right now your civilization is located on a created slice of time that is pulsating with an exquisite frequency potential.

As we share our stories and tales of trials and tribulations, no doubt you are reconsidering who you are, what you have lived and chosen to experience, and what you have embraced or have avoided. Ideally you are considering your own potentialities that manifest with marvelous originality in the opulent flow of unpredictabilities, which hold a purpose connected with all of existence. As you reflect on your life, rest at ease knowing that everything you encounter within your own tales is for a purpose. "And to what purpose can it be?" you ask. "And how can I experience something blatantly in front of me, and not be able to see it?" The answer is frequency modulation, as well as your intent and expectations and presumptions about reality. Within the great cycles of your cosmic calendar, the tests are the same, and the testees are you, returning again and again to manage one of the most difficult frequencies in existence: third-dimensional reality. And as 3-D reality becomes topsy-turvy and chaos becomes the new dance over the land, it is time for the vision you create to take root. Remember, thought is the vehicle through which you will learn how to fly.

In order for you to gain the best of experience, the highest of probabilities, and the most original of creations, you all must play your part, for we cannot build your world for you. You are in a coalescing phase now, deciding what your vision for the future will be, and this is imperative as you build the bridge and then traverse it, walking into a new slice of time— a new millennium in your terms—and opening a new age of experience on the great calendar of existence. As you proceed, allow yourself to have a greater definition of the future as we inspire you to have a vision. Remember, our vision is not yours; however we do see the possibility of you building a solid foundation from which you will reach a peak experience of living.

You have, metaphorically speaking, been to the top of the mountain and now realize that it is a big world, a huge cosmos, and an enormous existence, yet your seconds, the ones that have gone by and the ones yet to come, are also significant, each small second. A second can be sliced like a piece of fruit or cheese, and you will learn that as much exists inside a second of time as outside it. A small part can hold the wonder of all things, if you learn how to locate the code, the key, and the frequency from which to experience it. Everything exists in everything else, and you are destined to comprehend this.

The journey from density to great light is unpredictable,

and that is one reason why so many beings cluster here. Your point of existence in time is now a nest, a home of pure intent, comparable to a vein of gold miles wide, a phenomenon that perhaps would cause you to reappraise the value of gold. What if a massive vein of gold actually existed for a little while, then slowly disappeared? How would humans treat a fifty-mile-wide vein of gold running the length of South America? Would gold still be valuable? Would you hoard the site or build fences around it, or would you keep it a secret, if you could?

We use this example as a metaphor for the fleeting moment, the nanosecond of twenty-five years, where you are so privileged to live, achieve, and create—with awesome unpredictability—whatever you want. Events of this nature have their chapters in the Book of Existence, yet the Book is not made up of chapter after chapter of these kinds of opportunities. Time is relative, distinct to location and frequency, but then frequency is location. As we have suggested, in the address right next to yours, a slice of a second away, a parallel world can exist, one that you have been seeking to discover and explore for diverse reasons. Some of you seek to explore the mysterious world of dragons and lizards because you deeply relate to the subject, and even though these tales are told as myth and fairy tale, you secretly know they are real because you can feel it. Some of you are quite comfortable with these recollections while others are ill at ease because, although your feelings may seem unfounded, insane, and ridiculous, you remember something! Rest assured, dear friends, that however you relate to these old mythologies, the tales from your ancestors' experiences run rich in your blood, so relax.

In the vision of the world you can enter, and we particularly say "can enter" because you have many options, the fleeting moment appears to be cordoned off. Ideally this is for your own protection. When you are cordoned off, it is indeed a difficult test, for then you are on your own, uninfluenced. Perhaps, in this period, even the moon shall disappear from the sky, or other orbs of light will be born. The story is different for every chapter in the Book of Existence on just how the golden nuggets, as places of immense richness and opportunity for awareness, evolve. All of this is still being studied. As humans you are enamored of your telescopes, using them to look into space and observe how universes, stars, and black holes are born. Many of you are fascinated with this phenomenon, yet the nanosecond—the fleeting moment that you live within—is far more exquisite than the birth of a universe, because a so-called mustard seed in existence is changing all of the other seeds. A universe is reseeding itself through a small portion of itself, which was held intact just in case its own existence might be threatened by shifts and changes of cosmic weather, drought or pestilence, or separation and disconnection from the grandness of itself. In case that ever occurred, a plan within a plan within a plan was tucked away so that nothing would ever be lost.

On the Internet of existence, there are many files: Games, codes, and master numbers can be utilized to gather an extensive view of multiple realities in order to become participants within these realities, not merely button punchers sitting in front of a screen. The purpose is to experience a new way of living by redialing frequencies, and understanding that the part cannot be separated from the whole and that the whole is offering a glimpse of itself to a very remote and sequestered vein of gold, to you humans now.

If a vein of gold fifty miles wide and the length of South America really existed, then certainly there would be plenty of gold for everyone. However, a few may say, "Why would we give everyone plenty when some of us could have more?" Then, the matter of who would own the vein of gold and what to do with it would have to be considered. Perhaps some people would see that the real value was in keeping the vein intact, rather than dividing it, or building hotels there and offering tours, or selling off little chips of gold, marketing the vein whichever way possible.

Imagine that part of your existence, this twenty-five-year period, is like a vein of gold, enormously rich and vast; even so, in the Book of Earth and in the bigger Book of Existence, it is not easily found because existence itself is vast and the Book of Earth is hefty indeed. Each existing Book of Experience holds stories that weave patterns like a web, from one book to another. Suppose we were to show you the Book of Earth and you said, "We only have five minutes, what can we see in just one quick glance?" In order for you to comprehend its complexity, we would show you an exquisite tapestry, a weaving of colossal proportions, for then you could perhaps understand the importance of each thread of life. We offer this vista for your consideration and suggest you make it one of your cornerstones when you build your vision for the future.

It is essential for you to hold on to the vision of what you want to create, for you live in the home of intent, a place where many beings would be thrilled to exist, while others would kick and scream to the other end of existence to avoid going there. Remember, cosmic legends speak of you as humans curiously tucked away and sequestered in a slice of time in a certain location of frequency in a galactic spiral of the Milky Way, in precisely late-twentieth- and early-twenty-first-century Earth—not easily found, and yet you are living so profoundly.

Everything is connected, and showing you the Book of Earth in this capacity allows you to see the foundation of richness from which you spring: the threads of gold, of light and darkness, woven together to tell a lavish and true tale of your potential, as humans, to create by default or by decree. The vision you are forming is a result of understanding that power is energy, and energy is yours to use as a tool for responsible living into the next age of experience. The legends are full of your victories. You must hold a vision of the highest mind, understanding that it is the sum total of who you are, one humanity, that allows you to be linked up as a community. We look in the Book of Existence and see how others have accomplished a similar task, for the subject is studied, just as you study the skies searching for stars being born, and for super-novas and comets appearing. Your scientists investigate celestial phenomena, looking to find the once-in-a-lifetime event, unaware that where you are and what you live is the most spectacular event of all! You are unique, and yet you affect everything; it is highly unusual that a place so common, so seemingly harmless, and insignificant, should suddenly be the focal point of all existence.

The closer you move to 2012, the more all of existence will be abuzz about your location. Where is Earth? Is it happening? The legends have said that Earth is awakening, and you may wonder how can this be, that Earth will awaken. As you move further into the visions of your potential future, perhaps you will see yourselves becoming time-jumpers and time-travelers, fulfilling your destiny by journeying into all of existence, reassured that you have birthed your version of the frequency of love. This is a potential vision for you to consider. We also remind you that you are the creators at this time. We ask you therefore to create with compassion, originality, and courage, and to use the great geyser of energy that flows through you for positive change. Remember, augmenting this process of change is a natural unfolding of your psychic abilities, which will link you to multidimensional experiences that may appear at times to be like bizarre snips of movies. Do not be frightened, yet learn to be discerning and to assess the situation.

In addition to the encoding in the heavens that occurs as modulations of light, modulations of sound are also to be considered, some of which are audible and some not. Your world is filled with sounds of chaos, and as you become more psychically sensitive and in tune, you will feel more sensitized to sounds, and yet you may not always understand what is occurring. The DNA in your biological structure, and the multidimensional DNA that connects you to your expanded identity, are designed to unfold within you, just as the seed of a plant or a flower is designed to follow a pattern of growth, and does not have to ponder over the ability to complete its cycle. A seed holds a blueprint and, with the proper environment, it is destined to fulfill its purpose to grow and reseed itself, and to experience the struggles of casting away its casing, shooting upward through the soil, and then bearing the elements of sun, wind, and rain, as well as the scorching heat, flooding waters, and infestations of conquering insects. This is the experience of growth. When the plant blossoms, it experiences its own aspect of sexuality and produces its flowers, exquisite in their uniqueness, which herald the greatness of the fruits to come. The plants freely give their fruits so that you can live, and this is an interesting thought for your reflection.

Your DNA coding is layered in such a way that you will naturally unfold, and if you desire to bring forth or enhance the fullness of your own DNA, then we suggest you deal with life and give thanks for the foods you have, for the people who are part of your life, and for the family from whom you spring forth, both light and dark. Embracing your existence seeds your frequency into the ethers, and this in itself seeds the Earth, building your future. Many people have turned their backs on their families, and we see that those who have abandoned their bloodlines, no matter how justified it seems, have often missed the greatest opportunities to heal their ancestral lines through their DNA. In the Book of Earth, this lesson is repeated again and again when people shun what they do not like, or what they judge and find too difficult or fearful to deal with. In your world, a great cluster of people avoids doing the most difficult task again and again out of fear.

Your specific future goals are for you to decide, and we do remind you that exquisite possibilities exist. Your genius is at hand, and to really integrate living with one another on Earth, purposeful living must be established. So we ask you, to what purpose do you awaken every morning and go about your lives? Reflect on this thought for a moment, and do not condemn, judge, or applaud yourself for your present involvements, because whatever they are, they will change. The season of change is upon you, and wherever this change may take you, it is most important that you lay a foundation in the home of your intent, as a personal vision connected to a community.

You are confronted once again with the same old dilemma of the evolving genetic experiment. When will one of you look up and point to the sky, realizing that you have been looking at the ground all this time? Now is the time, and as we imagine it, we see that soon you will, most certainly, look up. Rest assured that what you experience is layered as a preparation for the new phases of growth. The tomato plant does not shoot up three or four inches and then declare, "I do not know how to go any further." In a crisis a plant may sometimes die, but hardly do all plants die; in general a built-in fortitude allows the plant to live through the drought or bend with the strong winds, to stand straight in the great heat of the afternoon and dig deeper to absorb more water. Some of you worry that you do not have the stamina to survive, so you rush out to be fixed and remade; yet all the potions, magic, and wizardry in the world can hardly accelerate the encoding that naturally unfolds in you. If you have been running around in circles of late, looking for what you think is needed for the next phase, then stop for a moment, find a place to relax and lay to rest your quivering and quaking.

It is time for you to understand the power of your mind —the individual mind, the global mind, and the galactic mind—and to realize that your unfoldment is awaited, just as you await the stars peeking out from the heavens reassuring your world that the heavens move in order, even though too many of you ridicule the meaning of that order. No matter what your logical mind tells you, the movement of the heavens humbles even the most arrogant of humans, and if you are not awed by the heavens, then you are a fool indeed like the emperor with no clothes, self-entrenched and self-enamored in delusion. Such is the nature of the test in all realities: to discover what is truth, and what is real, and where it is real. Now, here is something else for you to ponder: Where is this version of reality real? Versions have their homes, as you are learning.

In the vision you build for yourself, it would suit you to imagine that the changes and innovations, and the unfolding of who you are, will be experienced in such astounding measures that it will seem as if you will live, in your terms, many more years than you actually do. Multiple lifetimes may be encountered in a week because the more you learn, so much more gets pieced together, and then your threads will begin to weave their own tapestry. If we could show you for five minutes the tapestry of Earth before the finish of this time period, it would be small indeed; however it grows in size and significance because, as you unfold, you will connect with other time lines, and then you will understand simultaneous living. "Yes," you are saying to yourselves, "that's a good one! Simultaneous living. How am I going to manage simultaneous living when I'm having difficulty managing linear living?" Once again, the unfoldment is encoded in your body if you would, like the plants, trust the process.

The immense flood of energy that moves through your body wants to enliven you and connect you to others, but it is most essential for you to relax your body for this to happen. This heightened flow of energy can restore and enhance you, as well as make you feel jittery, nervous, or wired—as if you stuck your finger into an electrical socket. The choice is yours. It can also make you feel very heavy, where getting out of bed, just making a move from the covers to the bathroom, seems too much of an effort. You can respond to these changes by using your will to direct the energy toward what you desire, by acknowledging how you feel and where you are at in your life, and by knowing that sometimes your finger is in the electrical socket, and you are moving boulders at the same time! Identify these periods and do not judge yourself for being whoever you feel like that day. You are dealing with complex and profound energies: cosmic and earthly energies, energies that you produce as frequency broadcasters, as well as all of the stray energies in your world—inaudible sounds, microwaves, high- and low-frequency electronics, and the frequency modulation of your computers and satellites.

One of your visions for the future can be to create a utopian existence where light and dark harmonize, where all is allowed and yet all is respected, where rules are not broken because they are agreed upon, and where a unity of sorts exists. If you could achieve that vibration on Earth, it would be a valuable and priceless creation in the annals of time, carefully treasured and cherished. It would act as a signaling frequency, a satellite of sorts—like your moon is a satellite placed there to modulate you. Some of you are insulted by the idea of anything influencing or controlling you, and when you make such a discovery, you want to send off a missile or a spear to kill it first, and then examine it later. Killing simply sets you up for the same destructive vibration, for what you put out is what you receive. The creator must know its creation and cannot separate itself, and as creators you are part of the Maker's generosity and must also learn that you cannot separate yourselves from your creations.

If you were living in another slice of time, in another age, as another aspect of your ancestral multidimensional line, then you would not necessarily need to know all this. Perhaps in another lifetime it would be impossible to achieve such an understanding because the cosmic weather, the age, the frequencies, the mass consciousness, and the rate at which the genetic experiment would be growing, would not reach the necessary level of encoding. Imagine how you would feel if someone set you in a laboratory and said, "Here is a tomato plant and a beautiful lily; now use these two plants as inspiration to design and create a plant on your own." What if all of humankind had to pass this test in order to qualify for the next state of being? A new plant. How would you go about creating a new plant to contribute to a community? This too is something to ponder, to imagine for the future.

When you contemplate the future, do you envision that you will terminate at some point, or do you reach that mysterious place of immortality? Whatever your aspirations, the future will be different than what you imagine; it always is. Whether you live forever or die and live again and again, you will always encounter other versions of yourself. You seed the future and create it as your children and grandchildren, your "ancestors" of the future. You have forgotten this great great teaching: that the part cannot be separated from the whole, that you return again and again so carry this vision into your future. This is a strong, founding substance of creativity.

And speaking of creativity, it is the speciality of your ancestors, the ancient elders, the legendary lizards and dragons, or at least it was or has been or will be: Everything is simultaneous so it depends on which book, which frequency, and which Now one is viewing. Geneticists, designers of solar systems, and designers of galaxies all have creativity in common. If it was reputed that a birth was to take place in the heavens and you were a curious modern, you might view the occurrence and think, "Oh, look at the balls of light bursting forth," never imagining that you were watching the beginning of a designed, engineered project brought into form by the legendary lizards and dragons, that you were actually watching their creating. Myriad beings view the Earth as well, waiting because you, too, will be creating either wittingly or

unwittingly. Ideally, with the energies present—the signals
and signs, the symbols and feelings, the impulses, imaginings,
and the groundswell of intuitive knowledge that cannot be
stopped—you will read the winds of change, trust your feelings, and consciously allow yourself the experience.

Beings who have visited you and with whom you have
been enamored can sit back, over their expansive time spans,
and plan universes, galaxies, and solar systems because they
understand the creation principle. The recipe includes a little
bit of sound, imagining, trust, will, and intent, plus a purpose,
a plan, and a few more ingredients they have kept secret; however *there shall be no more secrets.* Your DNA is multidimensional
and is encoded to weave itself together to access the same
knowledge, as if all the water in every stream, lake, crook, and
cranny was suddenly compelled to connect with more water.
You, too, can be individual forms of uniqueness, yet still be a
knowing part of the whole that you will learn how to navi-
gate, seeing for yourselves that what you do here directly
affects what happens everywhere else. The dramas and challenges that you play out and solve here ripple across time,
particularly to the legendary lizards and dragons because they
await your solutions. In their ability to create, they have
become lost in their own creations, thinking that they could
create all of the universes, worlds, planets, and satellites, as
well as asteroids, that they could ride around existence changing and monitoring their own territory. And so your ancestors
became lost to the purpose of living—just as you have with
your ability to create gadgetry and electronics.

The legends on your planet are full of their visitations, of
the wars that other crusaders and visitors encountered when
they discovered Earth as time-jumpers. Earth is indeed a treasure, and it has been visited again and again. Now, at this
point in time, many beings are here and others wish to be here;
however a certain frequency is required to enter. The more
you rarefy your frequency, the more you will only at-

tract specific energies. Be wise in your choices, for fools are at hand as is always the case at a juncture of change. Snake-oil salesmen and charlatans abound, and some are impeccably designed to deceive, while others only deceive themselves with their own madness or perceived genius. You will see this parade of fools because the frequencies require you to be connected, for this is not a time of solitude. If you find yourself alone and without a friend, then make an intention to meet a new purposeful friend in the next few days, and do not put all kinds of preconceived requirements around this friendship. The great force of existence will often leave you gifts disguised in brown paper bags or wrapped in old newspaper, tied with a snip of shoelace, a bit of worn ribbon, or a dirty old string. Often you would pass them by for a finely polished person and miss the opportunity to build the bridge outside of your own belief system to link up as humanity. The importance of each person and their effect on the whole needs to be acknowledged, and this is encoded in your DNA.

As we have said, the understanding of genetics has already made a tremendous leap, although it is not common knowledge. Many discoveries kept from the public will be disclosed in rapid succession, and many of you will be astounded at how quickly you will have to readjust and learn new ideas. If these ideas had naturally unfolded during the last five hundred years, or certainly the last fifty years, it would be different and you would not have to expand now from a tight compressed state into such a wide-open existence. You would have been more gently prepared, so that when the full vista of living became apparent, you already had a peek at the vastness of the landscape. The process could have been designed to slowly open your awareness; however your response to life is different when you are quickly accelerated. As a species, you do have the capacity to accelerate beyond your conditioning, to absorb the shock of a sudden opening, of seeing through your belief systems, having to reconsider again and again a bigger and bigger picture—every day, month, and year. As we have said, if it seems like you are living hundreds of lifetimes at once, indeed you are! Although what you learn in the coming years may appear to be from this era, it is really a compilation of knowledge from all of your ancestors, from all of Earth.

In December of 2012, when you are poised on the brink of 2013, the time lines will open. There are those who have seen a few snippets of things to come, and think it will be this or that way. A vast canvas of possibilities exists: unpredictable, unprecedented, and of profound potential. It is the vein of gold we have asked you to consider, and the question remains: Will it be a jewel on Earth or will you moderns turn it into a sacred site or tourist trap? And please consider, what are the visitors thinking? Do they approach this vein of gold that you are as a sacred site, or will they set up their own franchise to convince you of their magic and to sell you your fortune or their own wares and ideas for your benefit? It is up to you to decide what to allow; you are, after all, that vein of gold. What are your intentions? How do you want to be viewed and experienced in the legends? These legends speak of renowned feats and of a total restructuring, reorganizing, reintending, and reexperiencing of third-dimensional reality; they tell of the rise of the human spirit achieving the impossible over and over again. The legends say you will reinvent everything through intent, will, love, and community—in the blink of an eye. It is through the reassurance, the love, and the support you have from one another that you will have your finest hour: the thirteenth hour, the hour of mystery, the hour that does not exist, the hour of the unknown.

Perhaps your greatest task in this moment is to trust. As you know, only you can make trust, only you can make yourself real, so turn off the chatter, the distractions of the outside world, and listen to the symphonies of Nature and seek to understand the power of sound on your being. Respond to

Nature with your own sound, your own melody or tone of intent, sending into the ethers what you want, your vision of the future. You may know that sound is a tool for creation, but you do not understand how powerful a tool it is. Each syllable that you speak, each vibration and tonality, has a different potential.

In your vision of the future, perhaps you will imagine a music that enlightens all people with sounds and songs you can remember, share, and pass down: songs of healing, of connecting, of exquisite wonder, songs of living and songs of sexuality with codes of meaning to strengthen the tapestry that all are a part of. When you think of the tapestry, recall it as a fleeting glance at a portion of the Book of Earth, as the image you can comprehend.

See if you can imagine a time in the annals of existence where the great reptiles, the legendary lizards and dragons, exist in cohabitation with you, a time when you were not being pillaged and conquered, or a time where you were not ignoring them or hiding in fear. Imagine a slice of time that shows you the potential of combining your skills and working together as exquisite creators. The legendary lizard mind is an exquisite creator, and in the Book of Existence and even in the Book of Earth, many tales tell of their deeds. As you seek to know yourself, go back to the most primordial source, the original creators—the most ambiguous, hidden, ancient elder ones—existing in what appears as a nonexistent slice of time, a nanosecond; yet it is there, in between your moments, that a place tucked away in the voids of time, but certainly full of landscapes of richness, is where these legendary lizards dwell. They now offer you a frequency—as if they were suddenly on the radio with their own show—a frequency they feel you can comprehend. They want you to remember them as magnificent creatures and allies, not as beasts to fear, but rather as friends who taught you to fly and traveled with you from one place to another, who were at your beck and call because to them you were so magnificent they simply loved you. They loved your abilities and your cleverness, your splendid beingness, the way you move your hands, the way your flesh ripples on your skeletal and muscular forms. They could not help but fall in love with you, and this they know you have forgotten. And so they ask you in your imaginings and reconsiderations, in your generosity, to remember them while looking in the Book of Earth, allowing a little bit of their reality to seep into yours for a few seconds, for a minute or two now and again. And in so doing, a little bit of your reality seeps into theirs, as is always the way.

They have something more to give you: They offer a vision of inspiration as a modeling species of intelligence, where different biological creatures are a result of each other's abilities to create, taking all their talents and building something unique from them. You have records of this occurring from when the great reptiles walked the Earth with humans. You believe the great reptiles disappeared sixty-five million years ago; we ask you to reconsider their extinction, for there is evidence that some great reptiles live even today. You have to learn to shift the dial of your beliefs. Perhaps you will travel to the end of the world, and even though it is round, you will find a way to fall off and perish in some never-never land of nonsense because you could not make the leap from a flat-world to a round-world view.

So we ask you, dear friends, to skip that human tendency to go screaming and wailing into times of change. Relax and be serenely graceful and develop a sense of humor. Hold on to your vision of working together toward a world of purpose. Imagine that genius is at hand, that it is coded and timed, and it shall be. Imagining brings energy into form and allows you to live, for the coding unfolds when you follow what excites you in an honorable way, when you connect with other humans, having a kind smile and standing up for yourselves, and understanding that violence is never the answer.

Purposeful clear living allows those who understand the laws to be the makers of reality. Understand that focus, will, and intent, directed by those who know, are the most powerful forces right now. The people who may seem to be after you, who harass and challenge you, do not really have a clue about these laws.

As a creator of your own experience, you must ask why you are choosing this reality. What lesson in living do you need to learn? It looks to us, in the Book of Earth and in all of the books we observe, that everything is an experiment; even the legendary lizards and dragons are part of an experiment, so do not think that you have been slighted or gypped because you have been made, and do not resent your Makers. It is time for gratitude. The reptiles, who want you to remember a creative kinship with them, can also show you mental pictures of a time thirteen thousand years ago, when your sun was halfway around the great precession of the equinoxes, in a time called the Age of Leo. That period, during the end of the Atlantean era, is in opposition to where you are now poised in this cosmic calendar, so you are very much connected and are relearning some of their lessons. In your vision of the future, remember the Atlanteans and their sudden, shocking, and surprising demise, and know that you will be challenged with the same lesson, though you will not necessarily create the same outcome. One repeats the experience to learn the lesson, not to create the same outcome again and again. Ideally, when one learns the lesson as an individual, a community, a world, and a galaxy, one changes the outcome of the experience. Then dramas need no longer be replicated, whether it is the same old pattern in your life or in the galaxy and the cosmos: divide-and-separate, fear-over-love.

You must trust your own biology, and that the rays of the sun, the comets, the planets, the stars, the wind and water, and the air, fire, and ether are as coded and purposely planned as the tomato seed and your own DNA. Embracing a sense of trust will assist your vision to grow from moment to moment, allowing in new ideas of what you would like the world to be. This vision is imperative. It has room for all people, young and old, all colors, and all species as well. In this age you will discover that you are all creators: six billion teachers, six billion Gods. What will you do with your creation? It is the weaving of these threads that now concerns you. What will you do with all of them? Everyone wants their thread in the tapestry, and goodness gracious, who is going to design the outcome so it is not a big tangled mess? You can hear it now, the artisans bickering in the back room as if they were working for a royal family, commissioned to portend some great event, gathering all the weavers, spinners, and designers together; yet no one can quite agree because everyone is a master and must have the most recognition. This has happened before and will challenge you again, yet you will find a way to blend their talents because everyone is an equal in this process.

Hold on to all of these visions, especially the vision of the legendary lizards and their impact on the Atlanteans. See if you can time-travel through yourself to these places of knowing. If you can open up to the venue of simultaneous living, you will change to become more you, yet the change will not entail dropping your identity and altering who you are; it is about becoming integrated, blossoming, and bringing out hidden facets, and connecting deeper with family, community, friends, and yourself. This form of change will allow room for simultaneous living to be in your consciousness, and the working of it is built into your biology. As we have said, you are more magnificent than any computer you will ever design; and as the designs of technology exceed the most radical and revolutionary discoveries, know that they are mirroring the encoding in yourselves, layer upon layer, bringing to the surface your abilities for healing, living, and creating.

In your imagination hold the vista of your life, your

world: the family and community with which you want to be joined. Send the image both inward and outward from this moment, knowing that it will pass everywhere and draw its own likeness, that it will vibrate off the Earth and with the Earth, and the Earth will reflect this signal outward as well. No technology will supersede this process because no technology can supersede the greatness of your own biological spirituality. So trust the process, dear friends, and allow it to unfold. Majesty is yours. Feel connected and create the ultimate community where you are proud to be graciously connected to Family of Humankind.

To Outmake the Maker

We ask you now, as an adventurer and journeyer into realms of understanding and mystery, to extend yourself into the depths of unfathomable antiquities. Relax your being and reaffirm your identity, then follow along through the words and the vibration of energies we share as we weave the purpose of this tale. Truth is a very important element of living and is relative to one's perception, location, and ultimately to one's point of view. If we have shared something with you that rings of truth or the lack of it, that is of course for you to decide. Our tales and lessons in living are in many ways for ourselves; we introduced ourselves as travelers and storytellers asking you to join us on this journey because, as we have learned, like attracts like.

You are, at this point in time, concluding many phases of your experience. Perhaps you have felt the need to withdraw, to move back in order to assess the panorama in front of you. We have spoken to you as Pleiadian journeyers and ancestors, and we have used the Book of Earth to help you locate yourself and to be prepared in some way for the momentous and extraordinary change that humankind is about to undergo.

We have viewed portions of your story as proclaimed in the books of your history, and through using the Book of Earth, we have explained to you the importance of your ancestors, that each and every moment of their lives makes up the Book of Earth. We have conveyed to you the essence of a book that is not easily read nor widely published, a book that is a treasure, one that requires a certain focus of consciousness before it can be understood. The Book of Earth holds the true living portions of each of its contributors, and its most interesting facet is that it cannot be read without it being experienced.

When you study the stories of your world, you do not in general experience them, you only read about them, and to a large degree you are uncertain of which stories are true and which are fabricated, which are official and which are unofficial stories. You call your stories history, and they are full of conquering, dividing, fear, and separation; however they are only one fraction of the time line, although a strong fraction indeed with deep power and even deeper secrets. The nature of your situation is to discover that deep secrets, hidden stories, and plans are stored all around you: in the ethers, in your bodies, and in the airwaves. Some of these plans may seem ominous: layers of frequency grids in the etheric or electronic grids built by satellites surrounding your planet as if to create an electronic quilt in space, a frequency fence perhaps. To what avail? Now that you understand that everything is frequency, why would a frequency grid exist in space around your planet?

One of the lessons we learned as journeyers is that the Makers, the designers of what we all experience, are vast indeed. And search as we would, we have not yet located the address of the Primary Being, All That Is, God, First Cause, Great Spirit, Goddess—whatever term you choose. The Maker appears to be invisible and holds its own hidden secrets, which continue to entice us forward, because as Pleiadian seekers we contemplate the consciousness of the designer. We have been humbled, truly humbled, in our journeyings and adventures, and we have been profoundly affected by what we have learned. There was indeed a need for a great alteration of our own collective consciousness before we were qualified to read the Book of Earth, for as we said, to study this book is to live it.

"How," you may wonder, "can this occur?" It is a good concept to ponder at this time, and if you really want to know the answer, then do the living that living requires, trusting that living with clear intent builds the frequency that qualifies you to know more. In knowing more, you really seek to meet with the Maker whose mysteries are untold, and yet all paths, it seems to us, lead to the Maker, even though as we said, the Maker has no address. The Maker moves all of the time, like some unfathomable spirit: here one moment and gone the next, just around the corner or just having left for the next town, or just having climbed over the mountain—elusive, evasive, ephemeral, and certainly mysterious and secret. We sometimes chuckle in our own Pleiadian journeyings and say, "If we met the Maker, then that perhaps would be the end of our journeyings."

You are living in auspicious times—interesting times most certainly. To fully grasp the opportunity that you have created for yourself is what we ask of you now. Imagine that as an artist you are given the opportunity to use the tools of the Maker. In your imagination on the screen of your mind, focus on your pineal gland and see your third eye open. Imagine that you are to paint a picture, an illustration for the Book of Earth. How would you capture the concepts from the stories and tales we have shared with you? You would, of course, incorporate all of the feelings elicited by you, knowing that your responses and reactions, consciously or unconsciously, contribute to the frequency of living and to the planet, and hence to the Book of Earth itself. How would you bring all of these concepts into artistic form? Picture it now, using your imagination and your pineal gland to see how to illustrate the Book of Earth; then perhaps, you would be qualified to read it, if of course you would dare. It is one thing to hear the tales and quite another to be one with them and to live them. Perhaps now you know how we know what we know, and perhaps you too will begin to grasp, in your ponderings, the mystery and the magic of the Maker as well. We have said that a creator cannot be separated from its creations, and that it is always best to start with the truth and end with the truth; and yet truth, as you are learning, is dependent upon where you are and what vibration you are experiencing.

As you step back and assess your new worldview, your new personal view, and certainly your new cosmic view, what does it all mean to you? Can you see the value in living? We ask this question of you as kin, fellow journeyers, and travelers. In our journeys, we certainly discovered eons ago that there was a value and purpose in living, and we also discovered that *one really cannot escape living.* In 3-D living appears separate from dying, and since much of your existence is physical, it therefore appears that life beyond death is nonexistent. However, peeling away the layers of your consciousness and revealing the panoramic view humankind is called to acknowledge will certainly shatter a few nerves. Sometimes, when a collective nerve-shattering experience occurs, a collective healing of profound magnitude can also be experienced, because normally the breakdown of your collective conditioning is extraordinarily difficult to accomplish.

You are resilient beings programmed eons and eons ago, and the ancient ones held their battles and fought through space for you. Feel into the unfathomable depths of space where something very ancient dwells, where forces beyond human—or beyond any form—can produce form and seem so intelligent and massive that you would consider yourself an insignificant insect next to them. Yet you are a result of their creations, and the creator cannot be separated from its creations. No matter how humble you may appear to the power of this intelligence, you are, nonetheless, encapsulated in its whole.

Your finest hour shall soon be upon you, and there will be an exquisite uniqueness to it. However, for now you have one more opportunity to reflect and go deeper inside yourself, to see what secrets your cells hold. In the Book of Earth, we have seen again and again that those who truly understood the value of the genetic data they held in trust here have always kept it secret. The maintainers of your world, in the employ of some of the designers themselves, were often in the dark or ignorant of your capabilities, your potentialities. Compartmentalization. You use the same process in your world and call it the chain of command, where a few know all, and the farther away you are from the source, the less and less you know of the experience.

As we have explained, this happens because you have abdicated your psychic abilities, which would allow you to read energies and know more. Some of you cannot even imagine, even at this point of our journey together, what "knowing" is. There are those of you who know, yet even with knowing, you can think you know, and still not know. Knowing is tricky. Knowing is like having some great new toy that keeps changing, that has its own consciousness. Who is doing the knowing? What is this process of knowing? How does it work, and why does it work? Where and when does it work? Knowing has been renounced by you or at least frowned upon most definitely, because if you *knew*, then you could not be managed so effectively. And those who manage you do not know either, for if they could feel your lives as we do in the Book of Earth, they would interact with you in a different way.

Once you immerse yourself in the vastness of creativity, you become what you make. If you sculpt, you become the marble, the clay, or the bronze. Ideally, as a creator you become the words and the paper if you write. If you produce life and take the role of mother or father, you feel and become the life of your offspring. This is, of course, the Maker's ability. Perhaps the Maker cannot be located because of being too busy making everything, or perhaps the Maker is waiting for this portion of creation to become one with the creator further down the line. Even though the time lines close down the closer you move to 2012, at one point they then finally become wide open. Eventually, everything that you are, and the whole world around you, can and will exist in simultaneous living— that enigmatic state that none of you have quite yet mastered.

The ancient ones, the legendary lizards who battled through space for you, their story is vast indeed and to read their book is quite a tale in itself. We see their tales weave in and out of the Book of Earth, like vacant tracks or slithers in the sand, leaving markings but no sightings. The books that you write are devoid of their stories, yet if they are brought into form through your words, then the believers know, the knowers know; however those who do not know are truly, as you say on your world, "clueless." Knowing has a season and is actually electromagnetic availability, and in your panoramic view of the Book of Earth as you perceive it, you will need to include this factor. Knowing takes courage. It can be freely given but not so easily kept. It can be weightless, and yet the densest and heaviest energy you would ever hold or pass through. Many turn their backs on knowing, and some run the other way. Some have no idea what knowing is, not the foggiest clue as to the experience, the being, and the oneness with knowing and what that really is.

In our vision of existence, we have the flexibility to remap time. Perhaps it is beginning to dawn on you that you have this ability as well. This does not mean we destroy time lines; it means we seek to remap and redesign reality, to arrive before the departure, so to speak, to thread ourselves through frequencies and the force of existence—the raw material of the Maker—and to use this source in a vastly creative, substantive, supportive, and serviceable way. This is our vision. We are the builders and creators in our genetic line—extraordinary builders. We have strength, versatility, and longevity, and a great abundance of creativity and humor. In our vision, we include a blending of talents and harmonies, one that encompasses multiple time lines where frequencies can be seen as streets and where new ways of travel will be understood, where time unfolds like a fan and the arrival precedes the departure. Our vision includes your vision as well, because you are connected to us, and it is as kin that we reach across time and space to you. However, in actuality, we really jump the nanosecond and the electromagnetic spectrum and are not far away at all; yet because you do not know how to travel in this manner, it appears as if we are located an imponderable distance from you.

The widening panorama of existence that you imagine in your mind occurs now to people all over the globe, as more and more humans reconsider their concept of living. Many are moving around in despair, which is exactly how some of the makers of some of the plans want it to be. Because of your current mode of living—your industrial, military, and political disconnectedness to each other and to Earth—you are activating certain biological codes that were planted in the genetic library of Earth to be triggered if and when Earth and her inhabitants reached a state of imbalance. These codes and master numbers—programs in your terms—were designed and implemented eons ago, perhaps billions of your years, in the unfathomable depths of antiquity where the legendary forces can travel, and which they sometimes call home and can certainly have their creative studios. From that depth were you designed.

How can that be? you wonder. How could beings, existing perhaps billions of years ago, design and plan biological responses in genetic codings for events so far removed? This too is something for you to ponder. How can that be? The computations that your computers perform today were unfath-omable to you fifty short years ago. And perhaps the technol-ogy from fifty years ago, hidden from you by the World Management Team, was far far in advance of what you were told. The same is true today, and this is part of the leap you will be required to make. Instead of experiencing the gradual discoveries leading up to many of these fantastic high-tech creations, they will be, as we have mentioned, thrust upon you at once—like the hidden technology to electronically ma-nipulate you and use you as a money source that has been kept from the public. There is not one country or place that has been exempt from this manipulation; it is sad news, and it is true.

In your questing, adventuring, and journeying, we do not share this news to bring you into despair. Part of our pan-oramic, multidimensional view will show you that every-thing exists in contrast and duality, certainly in the place that you call home; this is the way in which you discover what and who you are: through opposites. You do not need to an-nihilate or neutralize the opposites in order to know the whole; the sad truth is that in renouncing knowing, what could you then know? As we said earlier, one of the truths we have learned is that the part cannot stay separated from the whole. In allowing managers to separate you, you have suc-ceeded in separating yourselves from the Earth, your fami-lies, the very cells in your body, and from the significance of living. Everything is isolated, so you are to be congratulated as humankind for living out the experiment and making such a successful success of meaningless living. You have shown it can be achieved, volunteering to show that the part can stay separated from the whole. It is as if you have said, "Watch us take it to the extreme, where everything is unconnected, even the cells of our being. We will choose to live in an ex-periment where we are totally meaningless—although only for a while." That is the phrase at the bottom of the contract that your spirit and soul signed in the P.S. clause. So now, "only for a while" is ideally ending.

We have spoken of ages and the tests of an age, and we also mentioned the wealth of an age. As we see it, the true wealth of an age comes with your ability to shift your perception, and the test of an age embodies your choice of frequency—will you choose to produce the frequency of love? In every age, where endings and beginnings are the bridges from one lesson of living to another, it is important for all of mass consciousness to assess the panoramic view, achieving the great summation. The cosmic winds, the solar flares, the Earth herself, and your DNA now create the season of change that you have the fortune to live.

Reflecting on your ancestors, the flatworlders, we can use them as an example. Their task was small compared to yours. As we see it in the Book of Earth, the time lines somehow map themselves together in this fleeting moment. As much as we would like to magnify and study them, to see what they do, it seems as if you humans go underground, like moles in their tunnel systems. You create something so intricate that even the greatest of time-jumpers and time-line travelers and even we, who dare to read the Book of Earth and live it as we read it, seem to find that the chapter runs short and pages are missing. We know that in this time you clever humans will produce some pages here. We have said that legends in the cosmos speak of you. Perhaps in understanding how the arrival can precede the departure, you will understand how these legends can already be spoken of, when you have yet to live them with all the freedom that you dare to take on, with all of the creativity and connectedness that you dare to scoop up for yourself, and with all of the courage that it will take to live the coding in your own biological being. You are clever, creative, and coded.

Perhaps those of you who can learn how to utilize the coding, as it appears in front of your eyes and in the core of your being and begins to enrich the events of your life, will have the courage to live the coding and explore some of the Books of Knowing. As travelers and journeyers, we will give you a tip here: Books are quite tricky you know. When we first began to discover these unfathomable antiquities, as collections of stories and tales and great gatherings of creativity— which are truly magnificent compilations of living—we did not quite understand what it was to open one, to touch it, and to read it, in your terms. So we were, in all honesty, battered about a bit. We had to pick ourselves up and dust ourselves off a few times; confer, whisper, and wonder what it was that we had stumbled upon in this great journey of discovery. Usually with humor and well-intended grace, we would proceed noble in spirit, sometimes feeling puny perhaps—yes even we, puny Pleiadians—awed by the majesty of the making and knowing that we would encounter.

We share this bit of truth so that you will not be intimidated by what awaits you. You too will be humbled indeed, for it is part of living, or so it seems. Perhaps in the humbling comes an awe for the value of living and for the designers, the makers, and the planners, and an awe for a plan that contains no mistakes and that weaves the dark and light threads together to create something of contrast and beauty. Your compassion will allow you to create a greater rendition of the panoramic view of existence, and then you will decide for yourself. When you take up the tools of the Maker and decide to be an artist intending to bring into form what you know, hold the form in the essence of your imaginative being and choose compassion as a tool. The Maker, if you are so privileged to meet, may not say, "Oh, this tool is the most essential." The Maker is clever and waits for you to discover and wonder: "Maker, Maker, why are your creations so profound? What other tools do you have that you use, Maker?" The Maker does not mind us sharing this information with you, and this is the truth:

Compassion makes a fine tool for creating.

Many many Books of Knowing exist, indeed: There are Books of the Planets, each with its own line; and then there are books of all kinds of knowings, about the different life forces and their creations; and there are books and books on each life form—the four-leggeds, the wingeds, the two-leggeds, and the creatures of mythology, legends, and mysteries. They all have their books. Remember, one can only read these books by living them. That is where knowing and compassion enter. There are more books in the Library of Existence than you can ever imagine, each one waiting to be experienced, each one a marvel of collections; but once again, proper frequency is needed to align oneself. Remember, like attracts like, and as you prepare to read some of the books of Family of Dark, then you have to liken yourself to the experience and become it, and yet not lose yourself in the likening. This is a trick best mastered for all journeys into knowing.

The energies that would tyrannize you extend through the depths of unfathomable space and time. So, too, do the energies that would love and support you. As we have said, in the Book of Earth the stories are woven side by side, each one often unaware of the other, each one part of a simultaneous plan hidden from the plan of the neighbor or relative; here Dark and Light, using the same substance and the same space, are unaware of each other, although both perhaps thinking they are very aware and knowing. And yet true knowing has never really come to you, not in that way. Your psychic perceptions and abilities are tidbits of little snippings, left over from the tapestries, yet still lacking a true strong thread and a thread-weaver. It takes a season of change to truly be able to live what you know and experience it through your being. Then you will know.

In the Book of Earth, it appears that the genetics of your being have been impeccably prepared for this time. We convey this to you again and again because, once again, we see that you teeter toward worry. As the tests become greater, you must understand that so do your strengths and abilities to meet them. You are not tested and challenged without the ability to rise to the occasion: to change, transmute, transcend, remake, remodel, and rebuild yourself. The programming and the management of your genetics have been great over the years. We said that you were difficult to break down. Your conscious minds are only partially appealed to because it is your unconscious minds that rule you. If you question this, then look at the size of your brain and see how much is utilized by the conscious mind: a small percentage, most often less than fifteen percent, sometimes as little as five, six, or seven percent. Your subconscious mind is an uncharted territory, holding hidden secrets of your connection to the cosmos and the ancestors, secrets to genetic programming—each coded for its own season, its own time, like the seeds, bulbs, and plants that you watch grow. The subconscious mind, the hidden territory, will indeed, in the thirteenth and finest hour, become known.

We ask you to understand that the change is beginning to occur, and a hidden plan will eventually come to light as the subconscious is integrated with the conscious mind, each knowing the other's territory, the other's forte. At the deepest part of your brain—the part where memory can be changed and stored, located, and augmented—at the brain stem, lies the reptilian brain, another clue perhaps to the invisible tracks of your ancestors. Once you activate the eye in your brain, the pineal gland, by continuing to visualize the numeral eight or the sign of infinity across your eyes, meeting between your eyebrows, more of what is hidden will come forward. It is most important for you to trust the process and maintain your own common sense and connectedness to others.

The process involves the dismantling of genetic perception, and you indeed have been in genetic perception—your genes are wired to perceive reality in a specific way. We say wired, but in actuality it is through frequency modulation from the sun and moon, and even from the center of the Earth. At this time you cannot grasp the vast creativity of the designers and creators because you yourselves cannot yet operate at this level. Perhaps this insight can stretch your concept of simultaneous living, and you can reach out with your awe, inquisitiveness, and capacity for compassion to other forms of intelligence, and literally feel, be, and know the designers of your world whose plans within plans are intricately immense. These designers do implement their plans from the ethers, from the invisible domains, into the visible and physical without the receivers of these plans having a clue as to their origin. Many so-called clever humans have buffed their nails and patted their backs at their own brilliance, never suspecting what really made up their biological beings and the influence of the celestial software that encoded them at birth. Yet all of this allows you to be influenced by designs that are not part of any religion or any of the god hierarchies as you know them, designs that are so enormous as to use millions of you at a time as pawns in a plan. Imagine that this is neither an evil force nor a good force; it is a creator. And even this type of creator, who could arbitrarily move a million of you with its plans—so you would think these were your own brilliant unconnected, compartmentalized ideas—would have a vast mentor.

We want you to understand how these elements are connected and, as we experience and read the Book of Earth, how essential they are. Now you know that when we speak to you of your world, it is because we have felt and lived it. That is one of the requirements of a true time-jumper. Visitors, frequency-hoppers, there are many; however a true time-traveler becomes one with the journey. That is how one can have the arrival before departure. Time-traveling and time-jumping seem like a very exciting vogue. When people are remote-viewing and traveling out-of-the-body and beginning to see that there is a whole arena of potentiality, we would remind you: It is essential for you to dream, so do not give up your dreaming. Cherish your ability to sleep and dream with a powerful pledge to continue; for if you give up dreaming, then you will be giving up living. Dreaming and living go hand-in-hand because dreaming is the creative garden in which you begin to exercise your probable rights, in which you do your artwork in the ethers. It is there that you decide which pictures you will crate up and bring from the dream world into what you call the real world: the truth, as you call it.

The ideas you catch and receive are ready to be brought into form right now. A renaissance of creativity that is yours in this fleeting moment also ripples throughout the corridors of time, where a renaissance of the creators is your experience as well. There are those who are also realizing, as you are, that you cannot be separated from what you create. *We outright ask you to create the frequency of love.* We have offered you suggestions for foundations and for visions. We have ideally shared with you an interesting commentary on your world, as we have shared our tales and tidbits with you from the Book of Earth. But the purpose of our tale is to relate to you the most important ingredient of all, the actual secret of the Maker: *Love*. The Maker is willing now for you to have that secret, and perhaps even in your own magnificent renaissance of creativity, you will outmake the Maker with love. The Maker chuckles at this idea, and as ethereal and ephemeral as it is, a chuckling goes out. The creations to outmake the Maker, that would be an interesting experience indeed, like the arrival before the departure. So we ask you to make the frequency of love. It is not always easy to ask for something, as you may well know, for many are afraid to ask because of a fear of refusal or rejection. Be that as it may, as your ancestors and kin, as ancient ones and experiencers of the Book of Earth, we ask you to make love because it is needed.

As we have said, some pages of the Book of Earth are missing, and that part of the tale, which no one can read with certainty, becomes more foggy and ambiguous the closer it gets to 2012. The more refined the frequency becomes, the less accessibility one has to meddle, mix, lobby, and mingle or even to observe; and as the mists roll in and the fog deepens, we get only a glimpse now and again, and how to put it all together even we cannot see. Your point in time simply shows pieces of a puzzle, glimpses through the mist. What it all means, why the pages are missing, we ponder this ourselves. However, because it is a fleeting moment, we are patient. We know we will be around to experience this fleeting moment, as ideally you will as well. We sit, if sitting is what you call what we do, and we await with anticipation and excitement, with profound admiration for our ability to place ourselves where we can observe such an event, where we can learn something about living that would enhance our own journey. We are very excited to see what you will do, how you will handle the test of an age, and whether or not you will recognize your wealth.

Are we meddling by asking you to produce love? Yes, perhaps we are. But it seems to us that all the books that make up the Book of Existence would benefit from your production of love. The legends speak of it and the legends run wide. No one knows the source of the legends about the humans in the late-twentieth- and early-twenty-first-century Earth, where it is said the golden moment is achieved and extended, where the nanosecond is designed to be, for a while, an eternity. Paradoxes, enigmas, flights of fancy, twists of fate, and stretches of the mind into the inconceivable, all of these await you. Perhaps by now you are envying the flatworlders, thinking that they had it easier, that at least the world they encountered was more known; yet it was really no more known than yours. A frequency change existed in the ocean waters, so to cross from one continent to another was truly like traveling to another dimension. The frequency of the dwellers in the new lands held different beliefs; therefore different manifestations occurred. The seeding of the belief is paramount to the ability of the manifestation, and as you believe, so it shall be. In order to create a new being, new beliefs are laid as a foundation and old beliefs, like the stones of antiquity, eventually crumble with time.

We remark on your flexibility and marvel at your own changeability, because if you have journeyed with us this far into the depths, into the hidden, mysterious scenes behind the scene and plans behind the plan, then you now are ready to know much more. The season of change is indeed upon you, a change imprinting you with a magnificence that requires you to produce the frequency to access it. Believe in yourself, for you are all artists etching the arena of living with your mind. Know that the fictions of the day bombard your consciousness electronically with official points of view, but hardly a news article or reporting really holds the truth, or at least the truth you are looking for, the truth that is not separate, the truth that connects you to all things.

Truth seekers you shall continue to be. As you seek the truth, time after time your bubble of innocence will burst, and you will find yourself on the ground like Humpty Dumpty perhaps, all cracked and bruised, perhaps weeping and saying, "I didn't think it was going to be like this. Goodness gracious, I thought life was something far more sweet and pleasant, and now I'm discovering all these distressing things." The distressing, disturbing, and disruptive experiences that may come your way may actually be there for you to heal them and not for you to feel wounded or affronted by. The wealth of an age is determined by your ability to shift your perception; remember that. The wealth you accrue will ideally encompass a healing vaster than any you can imagine. In seeking out this healing, it will happen in all of the bodies of your being. As a 3-D being this healing will occur in your spirit, which will be changed by the deep emotional transformations you are all required to experience now. After all, you are on the quest for knowledge, and to be able to know you must become one with all of life. So you must turn on your emotions now, your ability to feel, and recognize that imprints from childhood are coming to the surface so that you can realize that many of you are stuck in childlike behavior, because you were never taught how to use your feelings to perceive reality. Let go of your need to be mothered and fathered. Be complete. That does not mean to give up being a mother or father; just give up the idea of someone having to take care of you. Embrace the concept that you are sovereign and self-sustaining, and you will take care of yourself.

Lessons in living are vast, and the opportunity you have is immense. Some call it karma. Perhaps in those terms, you can understand that there are junctures and points of existence when you can release yourself from your own entrapments, and that as a creator you can only expect that you get back what you put out. On the vast stages of existence, this is what we await. So what you write in these final pages in the Book of Earth is up to you. We have our supplies and we are waiting, watching, and supporting you; we know that in those closing moments of the nanosecond, you will be meeting the thirteenth hour: the unknown, the mystery. Perhaps you have a few ideas of your own now and want to rewrite chapters yourselves. Perhaps you, clever humans, took those pages out of the book so that they could never be reexperienced again! We are learning much by observing you and experiencing your book, and yet still you are an enigma to us; so coded are you with magnificent flights of fancy and freedom to change that you are hard to plot. Yet you are creatures of awe and wonder, and we cannot help but love you.

So, dear friends, your own panoramic view will grow. Whatever artistic creation you bring into form today will unfold like a fan, and ideally the wealth of an age will be yours.

In the greater ideal, the test of an age will be achieved: the vibration of love, a gift to all of existence. Now, if you understand why you await celestial events—comets, eclipses, and full moons—perhaps you will understand why we await the event of you. Our experience, knowledge, and existence have been vastly expanded by your ability to live, and we ask that you continue to do so with style, dignity, grace, and purpose.

The depths of unfathomable antiquities call you to turn them inside out and to bring them to the light of day, to make them fresh once again. Your ancestors are willing to move forward from the ancient depths, knowing perhaps that they face their final days. They do this with grace because the legends are full of the rumors, the stories of the healing, the coming of the love frequency produced by the humble humans. Even the ancient ones will come forward for this event. The legendary lizards, the dragons, those who are a hidden part of the story, are now on the slow trek, too. They send their message: We are coming. The legends are full of this healing, and they hear it is occurring and that the humans are producing these frequencies in spite of all the tyranny and ominous toxicity in which they live. They are doing it! The word is out.

And so an ancient march is on. Beings that come from places that you cannot imagine, all trekking and journeying on their own pilgrimage or quest, because the legends say that in the Time of the Healing there has never been anything like it in all of existence. The time-jumpers, of course, tell these tales, and as we have said, time-jumping is an art, and you are only as good as your frequency and your daring to become what you jump into, and then not to become too likened to it; and then, of course, to extricate yourself, find your location and identity, and move along without necessarily getting stuck anywhere. But this happens, and the tales are also full of these stories.

Now in the final pages of your part of the book, the ancestors come to you in all forms and capacities: through the dimensions, through the Earth, through your blood and cells, and through the very water that supports life on your planet. An important pledge is for you to keep the waters safe and sanctified, and to understand that when the waters are out of balance, they are the ultimate signal that your activities on the planet's surface must stop. You can live through these poisonous toxic times and produce the love frequency; it is also your challenge to use common sense and to stop the production of this toxicity. You will do this as you all begin to feel much much more deeply.

In conclusion, dear friends, paint a grand panorama for yourselves and know it is the first of many. Masterpieces of life and its purpose will now be yours as humankind illustrates the great Book of Earth.

13

The Finest Hour

Perhaps by now you have concluded that this journey may not end. The pages you find yourself turning may turn you around to the beginning, because the end and the beginning are always most intimately connected. In your journeyings, you may find that in the end you arrive where you started so as to know the place once again. This has a purpose. You have a saying on your world, "history repeats itself." Any form of consciousness would continue to repeat its experience because it either so enjoyed what it was doing and sought out the experience again, or the consciousness was so unaware of what it was doing that it did not realize it was repeating itself.

As journeyers, travelers, and mystery seekers, we ask you to follow our words and turn these last few pages, and at the same time to consider very clearly all that we share. Shift your conscious mind and feel a mist—moist, wet, and ephemeral—swirling in the landscape around you. We ask you to step into the mist, into a place of mystery where you can see nothing at all, yet you feel the spaciousness. This in itself is a mystery: to be so enclosed and to see nothing around you, and yet to feel more expanded than ever. It is a trick of the mist, you know. Mists have been equated with "mystery"; they are one and the same in the old language of your world.

So step into the mist, into the mystery that awaits you, into the enigmatic, paradoxical, and certainly puzzling energies you are required to contemplate. In the mist, as you continue to feel it swirling around you, you find yourself moving forward. You feel a sense of trust as a force gently compels you onward. Uncertain of the terrain and totally unaware of your surroundings, you still continue to move along, and eventually a vague shape appears in the distance. You are drawn to this form and notice that it emits a light that changes color, but the light is so subtle it is difficult to pinpoint. You follow the mist, and the mist envelops you and you become one with it, using the mist to travel into what the mist knows; for the mist exists between you and the other worlds.

The shape and its changing light draw you farther into what looks like a vaulted cavern. Although you have wandered in the mist for a while, you wonder how you found your way to this place. As the mist begins to dissipate, to swirl around and rise upward, you see before you in the middle of this huge cavern a table of immense proportions. Once again you feel compelled to move forward as you step toward the table. A sense of majesty, excitement, and electrifying intelligence suddenly envelops you, and you now sense that the entire atmosphere in the cavern is electrically charged. In front of the imposing table are steps lined with a rich, opulent red carpet that is soft underfoot. Eight steps lead you upward to the tabletop, and there you find an open book of colossal and astounding proportions. The book's energy draws you toward it, and you find yourself using the pages as steps to scramble up to the top for a better view of this mighty book.

Now perch yourself in a comfortable position and allow yourself to enter into the Book of Earth, and whatever line of time you find yourself in, let the probabilities of that location teach you. The Book of Earth can be easily accessed now, so feel free to thumb its pages by simply thinking of various time frames or structures in your planetary history that interest or influence you, or places where you would just like to have a peek. Using your multidimensional skills, go deeper into the Book of Earth. Choose a time line and watch it unfold while we tell you about other lines of time.

On their own journey, in another line of time, spheres of light are traversing what you would call the universe. You exist on Earth, part of a solar system, part of a galaxy, yet these light spheres are part of the greater universe. You know of this universe, but as yet you cannot traverse it; these spheres of light can, and they are in search of something. Organic in nature, they house consciousness; actually these spheres house thousands of time-jumpers and time-travelers.

The spheres travel through the universe looking for the time of the legends, the Legends of Light. They search to find the pages in the Book of Existence where the Legends of Light and the Legendary Humans came into being. They enter the Book of Existence, which is about your universe, and they sit on its pages as you sit, in a similar fashion, on the Book of Earth. They converse amongst themselves as they pursue coordinate points, and they too have their own mist that they pass through to learn the secrets of these points in time. They have a way of reading space, of reading the ethers, and of merging their molecules around any molecules of tyranny that exist, to seek out the tyranny's basic imprint, its basic frequency codes. The travelers, in their organic spheres of light, are searching for the coordinate points of a fleeting moment in time. They are looking for a nanosecond in existence where, as they have heard, the Legendary Humans first arose.

These travelers come from a number of different systems. They are a time-jumping confederation of sorts, an official ex-

pedition through existence, time-jumping to find the exact
time and place where the legends are first born. They want to
enter to watch, and have journeyed far and under many many
conditions that would be beyond the comprehension of those
of you who simply understand the Book of Earth. As you flip
through the pages of the Book of Earth, imagine that a consciousness is flipping through larger pages looking for you.
The lines of time you seek to understand indeed precede the
moments in which you have lived; but lines of time also exist
from the future, for these spheres of light, these organic balls
of being, come from all different times. They are a confederation that seeks to be in the time and place where your stories
were birthed and made.

As you view the pages of your book to see what you can
learn and experience, imagine a much bigger book, the Book
of Existence, and the beings who watch you, who look to
jump into the fleeting moment and enter your reality to harmonize with its frequency—to watch and to be. Of course, because the fleeting moment is short, it is not so easily found.
Yet, since all time exists simultaneously and is like a video
loop that can be replayed again and again, the sphere travelers, on one hand, have forever to find the fleeting moment.
On the other hand, the longer they wait, the more the fleeting
moment can be redone, or perhaps the coordinates will slip
away, or perhaps those within the fleeting moment will miss
it entirely.

These sphere travelers were raised on the legends, and in
the worlds in which they developed, the stories they learned of
the Legendary Humans were about a genetic experiment.
They feel they know all about genetic experiments, and that
genetic experiments are tricky indeed but somewhat pre-
dictable. However the lines of time and jumping time are
unpredictable—extraordinarily unpredictable. And of course,
depending upon the venue or density, all kinds of ramifica-

tions and mysteries can occur. In the densest density of all, it is very difficult to operate, and yet in the search for all-knowing, if one wants to become all-knowing, one must experience and know all things.

So the searchers search, and in finding the coordinate points, they are ready to translate themselves so as to watch the big show. In the watching, each one of the watchers represents a different intention, species, and a different point of view. Each one understands that, according to the legends, a frequency is produced that is unheard of, and it occurs as a result of random chaos—which, of course, all the participants understand is a form of creation. Plans within plans within plans are really based on chaos, and the chaos that creates itself can be interpreted according to the point of view or the truth of the participant. And that is the richness, the wealth of chaos, which is thought to be one of the sweetest elixirs within love's retinue of existence.

So it is that these time-jumpers do not want to affect the chaos, and yet they do not want to be taken over by the chaos either. But the ambassadors in the spheres carry a number of legendary cosmic beings—family members, royalty of the snake clans and the dragon lines, the dragon kings—who come to participate in the healing, to be there to receive the frequency, to see if the legends are really true. In their time, the legends of the humans producing this healing frequency are so ancient, they wonder if they have the tale right. And because of events that have transpired on their worlds and because books have been lost and generations have elapsed, they decided to mount an expedition—at quite an expense and requiring a great deal of cooperation—to journey through time and the universe to invest in discovering an ancient fleeting moment. They want to see if the legends are real, that if in a place tucked away in an arm of the Milky Way, in a fleeting moment of time, human beings went from density to light, from fear to love, to experience something that, even as they spoke the words, these beings had no idea of what they meant. That in itself is the richness of the human chaos, and through chaos would they produce their ultimate gift, and it is *only* by creating chaos that it can be achieved.

And so the watchers, the visitors, the ambassadors travel through their book and they watch and they wait—for you.

Afterword

We trust that our work is appropriate. It is timely indeed and delivered with great love and a sense of purpose. We appreciate all of you who have read this book and who are now inspired to illustrate the pages of The Book of Earth with a greater sense of creativity, of wit and wisdom; to embody a renowned splendor, where you truly live the legends, the legends created with light. This is our intent in the delivery of this work, and it is our immense pleasure to participate in the restructuring of existence.

About the Author

The Pleiadians are a collective of extraterrestrials from the star system, the Pleiades. They have been speaking through Barbara Marciniak since May 18, 1988.

The Pleiadian teachings can be likened to those of shamanism, the ancient body of energetic knowledge that has served as intermediary between the realms of the physical and the spiritual, leading people to self-discovery in the worlds of paradox, paradigm shifting, and spirituality.

Barbara Marciniak is an internationally acclaimed trance channel, inspirational speaker, editor, and author who lives in North Carolina. She began channeling in May of 1988 in Athens, Greece, at the conclusion of a three-week journey through ancient Egypt and Greece. On this trip, Barbara was impulsed to reexperience specific temples and power sites in this lifetime—the Great Pyramid at Giza, the temples along the Nile, the Acropolis in Athens, and Delphi.

Since that time, Barbara has conducted class sessions and workshops throughout the United States and has facilitated tours to sacred power sites in Great Britain, Peru, Bolivia, Mexico, Egypt, Greece, Bali, and Australia. She feels that the sacred sites themselves are connections to energy vortexes that hold knowledge of the higher mind, the higher idea that Earth is presently seeking to re-create. Her travels, astrological studies, and a lifetime of alternative and free thinking augment her insight and understanding of the material she channels.

Barbara feels that her experience with the Pleiadians has been a gift of priceless value, connecting her with opportunities for personal, global, and cosmic transformation; and for this she holds tremendous gratitude.

For information on audio tapes, transcripts, and her quarterly newsletter, *The Pleiadian Times*, please send a self-addressed stamped envelope (for foreign inquiries, please include an international postal coupon) to:

Bold Connections
P.O. Box 782
Apex, NC 27502

BOOKS OF RELATED INTEREST
BY BEAR & COMPANY

LIQUID LIGHT OF SEX
Kundalini Rising at Mid-Life Crisis
by Barbara Hand Clow

MAYA COSMOGENESIS 2012
The True Meaning of the Maya Calendar End-Date
by John Major Jenkins

PLEIADIAN PERSPECTIVES ON HUMAN EVOLUTION
by Amorah Quan Yin

THE PLEIADIAN AGENDA
A New Cosmology for the Age of Light
by Barbara Hand Clow

THE PLEIADIAN WORKBOOK
Awakening Your Divine Ka
by Amorah Quan Yin

THE PLEIADIAN TANTRIC WORKBOOK
Awakening Your Divine Ba
by Amorah Quan Yin

VIBRATIONAL MEDICINE
New Choices for Healing Ourselves
by Dr. Richard Gerber, M.D.

Contact your local bookseller

~ or ~

BEAR & COMPANY
P.O. Box 2860
Santa Fe, NM 87504
1-800-WE-BEARS